The Most Helpful Traders on Twitter

By Steve Burns & Holly Burns

Contents

Disclaimer:

This book is meant to be informational and should not be used as trading or investing advice. The views, suggestions, and strategies of the traders featured in this book do not reflect the views of the authors, nor are they endorsed by the authors. No one associated with the creation of this book makes any guarantees related to the claims contained herein. All readers should gather information from multiple sources and create their own investment strategies and trading systems. Please trade responsibly.

Foreword

"Facebook is the people you went to high school with. Twitter is the people you wish you went to high school with." – @AdrianParsons

In 2012 I conducted a poll of "The Most Helpful Traders on Twitter" and asked my blog readers to contribute to their favorites. I like to follow people that are informative, funny, and add value to the community. I hoped that the poll would help all of us find new and interesting traders to follow. The response was great; there were many traders that were new to me and folks had fun with the poll.

I have continued to host the poll every year because it helps traders decide who to follow on Twitter. The voting process and resulting blog post have become one of the most popular features on NewTraderU.com, but I started to wonder if there was a way we could reach more people and spread the word about the Twitter trading community.

I decided to survey the top traders on the 2015 poll so readers could get more information about their process, trading tools, and psychology. This book is the culmination of those survey results. These traders were generous with their time and advice, and I am grateful for their friendship and participation. They are presented in alphabetical order, and the questions and responses may vary slightly for each entry. I think that you will find their responses to be informative and entertaining. I know I did.

Steve Burns

@SJosephBurns

@AdamHGrimes

Chief Investment Officer at Waverly Advisors Author of "The Art and Science of Technical Analysis".

Name:

Adam Grimes

Website:

http://adamhgrimes.com

Email:

adamhgrimes@gmail.com

How long have you been active investing or trading in the financial markets?

20+ years

What year did you become active on Twitter?

Services you offer:

I publish daily and weekly research and market ideas for traders in stocks, futures, and currencies, on time frames ranging from intraday to long term investing.

Which markets and instruments do you trade?

Stocks, currencies, futures, and options on stocks and futures.

Why did you choose these markets?

My trading style evolved over the years to cover pretty much all liquid markets. I find an edge in all these markets, though they require different approaches.

What type of trader do you consider yourself?

Swing Trader

Do you have a target for your average annual returns?

No

What time frame do you prefer to trade in, and do you ever change time frames?

Ideal time frame for me is 2 days to 2 weeks, though I spent many years daytrading and also do a lot of work on much longer time frames.

What is the maximum drawdown you are willing to tolerate in pursuit of these returns?

Depends on specific approach. 15% is a good target for some types of trading, but some (trend following) require much more willingness to endure larger drawdowns.

What technical indicators do you use to help quantify buy and sell signals?

I use Keltner Channels and a modified MACD, but these are secondary to the patterns that I trade. I don't use indicators to mark entries.

Are there any chart patterns you use for trading?

Subjective chart patterns can be useful, but I'm not sure you can build a reliable program on them. I've gone beyond chart patterns to quantify a number of other types of patterns in the market. These are patterns that you could see them on charts, but it's not at all what most people mean when they say "chart pattern". I think of my approach as a blended quantitative/discretionary approach.

What was your best trading year and what did you learn?

2007-2008 were good years. In those years, I learned that probabilities and patterns are reliable guides, even in market extremes. This time could be different, but it probably isn't.

What was your worst trading year and what did you learn?

Worst was when I started because I didn't understand risk and leverage. Switching markets/time frames also caused some bumps along the way.

How do you quantify your entry into a trade? What parameters do you use?

I usually enter on a breakout (i.e., with short term momentum) using what many people would consider a fairly wide stop (in the neighborhood of 3-4 ATRs on the trading time frame).

How do you manage your exit from a trade? What parameters do you use?

I usually exit part of a trade at a predetermined target, and then the rest on some type of trailing stop. I'll also add to a trade and finesse exit a bit more at times.

What is your favorite trading quote?

Most trading quotes are potentially harmful, especially the ones people throw around. "The trend is your friend." (only at times and only in certain kinds of trading) "Your first loss is your best loss." (Again, only in certain types of trading) "Only price pays." (Patently false and dangerous because it makes us ignore other *costs* (the flip side of "pay") of trading: volatility pays, time pays, carry pays, factors pay, relative performance pays if properly hedged, etc. It's hard to find trading quotes that apply universally.

"Know where you're getting out before you get in." – Bruce Kovner is one that might apply to almost everyone.

What are your favorite trading books?

There's something of value in every trading book, but I don't read many trading books anymore. The ones that go "bar by bar" I think are highly misleading. The market is noisier than that. It looks good in hindsight, but it can't really be applied in real time. I have a reading list on my website, and it's extensive. I think people should focus on building a strong background in finance, accounting, economics (even though most of those topics are minimally applicable to most types of trading), and a stronger background in statistics (essential). In most cases, trading books oversimplify. Time would be better spent understanding how to learn and understand the market.

Who are your favorite traders to follow on Twitter?

I find social media to be counterproductive for good trading. Twitter, in my experience, magnifies the emotions of trading, in a very negative way. Groupthink, hostility, pride, ego, all of these things are more important on social media. No one wants to hear what they need to hear (understand probabilities, manage your risk, you're going to be wrong a lot so move on, etc.) on Twitter. The quote I think of when it comes to finance social media is: "The best lack all conviction while the worst are full of passionate intensity" (especially the last part of that. :)

Who has influenced you the most on your trading journey?

I had several mentors who were essential to my success. Two were traders, two were academics, and one was an artist.

What lessons have the markets taught you about yourself?

Pride kills. You're going to be wrong a lot. Your emotions are highly misleading and will cause you to make errors. I tend to be very contrary, to the extreme, and I can't argue my positions with anyone or I get stupid. When I get stupid, I lose money. I need to separate the universe into things for which I am responsible and things for which I have no responsibility. The first list is actually quite short, and the second I can't worry about.

What lessons have the markets taught you about other traders and investors?

The crowd is not always wrong. The crowd makes certain reliable mistakes. Most people who try to trade will fail. Most people don't understand the market or what trading really is. Most people are not willing to do the kind of work it takes to be successful, over the length of time it takes. It's not about being smart; it's about doing the right thing.

What do you love about trading?

The fact you play a game where they pay you to be right.

What do you find to be the most difficult aspect of trading?

Returns are highly variable and not always clearly attached to actions. You can do the right thing and lose money many times in a row. You can do the wrong thing and make money. Your subjective sense of your performance is nearly always wrong.

What are the biggest mistakes that lead to a trader's unprofitability?

Doing things and using tools that don't work. The vast majority of tools traders focus on (e.g., moving averages, Fibonacci ratios, many chart patterns) completely fail to show any edge in statistical tests. If there's no edge, you can't make money using the tool. This is, far and away, the most common mistake; simply doing things that don't work. Being undercapitalized. Having unrealistic expectations with how long the learning curve is or what "success" looks like.

What one piece of advice would you give to a new trader?

You're going to lose at first, and maybe for a long time. Plan on that. Keep your bets small enough so you can lose over and over and endure the learning curve.

@Alexanderyf

Portfolio Manager. I use Elliott waves, Technical Analysis, Fibonacci, Daily market analysis and signals. Equities, Futures, Forex, Metals. Not investment advice.

Name:

Alexandros Yfantis

Website:

www.trading2day.com

Email:

admin@trading2day.com

How long have you been active investing or trading in the financial markets?

15 years

What year did you become active on Twitter?

Services offered:

SMS trade alerts on FX, Commodities, stocks, indices, CFDS, and futures from my portfolio. Greek stock market analysis. Analysis on demand. Clients requests my analysis on a specific product of his/hers choosing.

Which markets and instruments do you trade?

Major Forex pairs, Commodity and FX futures, index futures, index and stock CFDS, stocks in cash market, and options.

Why did you choose these markets?

Liquidity, popularity, ease of data access.

What type of trader do you consider yourself?

Swing Trader and Trend Follower

Do you have a target for your average annual returns?

No

What time frame do you prefer to trade in, and do you ever change time frames?

4-hour and Daily

What is the maximum drawdown you are willing to tolerate in pursuit of these returns?

-15%

What technical indicators do you use to help quantify buy and sell signals?

Ichimoku Clouds, RSI, Stochastics, Elliott Waves, Fibonacci levels.

Are there any chart patterns you use for trading?

Triangles, wedges, head and shoulders, channel breakouts, and hammer candlestick patterns.

What was your worst trading year and what did you learn?

2003, 2005, 2006, and 2015 were my worst years. I learned that I should always use stops and never get influenced and change my view because someone else has a different view. I shouldn't be influenced by others and should always stick to my charts and my analysis. I also learned to be patient because there were many trades I was right about, but because I rushed into opening a position, I also exited too early because the market was volatile and I didn't want to lose my early profits. I also learned to see each trade separately from the other trades.

What was your best trading year and what did you learn?

2010, 2011, 2012, 2013 and 2014 were my best years because I didn't repeat the above mistakes and always followed my analysis. Whenever I was wrong, my stops protected me.

How do you quantify your entry into a trade? What parameters do you use?

Most of the time when I enter a trade, I open a partial size and not a full size position. I take into account my stop level and I open a position that would not hurt my total account by more than 1%. I use stop orders to add/build on top of my position if my view proves correct. I add following the trend.

How do you manage your exit from a trade? What parameters do you use?

Fibonacci levels, resistance levels from previous highs or lows provide my targets to exit. I also exit positions if my stops are hit. Trailing stops are also placed to protect my profits.

What is your favorite trading quote?

"Everything you need to know is right there in front of you." - Jesse Livermore

What are your favorite trading books?

"Elliott Wave Principle" by Prechter and Frost and "Mastering the Elliott Wave" by Glenn Neely

Who are your favorite traders to follow on Twitter?

I have no favorite traders. There are a lot of people I value their analysis and view of the markets, but I don't follow anyone for their trades.

Who has influenced you the most on your trading journey?

The Internet, Twitter, the people I have talked to in forums, and the people I met and talked with in webinars.

What lessons have the markets taught you about yourself?

I've been taught to be more patient and always stick to my rules and analysis.

What lessons have the markets taught you about other traders and investors?

In order to be successful one needs to block emotions and sentiment.

What do you love about trading?

The ever-changing environment. Every trading day is different than the previous one and there is always something new to learn.

What do you find to be the most difficult aspect of trading?

Consistency. It's easy to make a profitable trade or two. The difficult part is to be consistently profitable and never let your losing trades take back all your profits from the other trades.

What are the biggest mistakes that lead to a trader's unprofitability?

Two of the biggest mistakes are trading without stops and trading bigger sizes than one can normally handle. Use less leverage, as the great Dale Pinkert sings in LAR.

What one piece of advice would you give to a new trader?

Have a plan, follow your rules, use a stop, and start small.

@Alphatrends

Chartered Market Technician, Stock Market Trader, Author of Technical Analysis Using Multiple Timeframes. Only Price Pays!

Name:

Brian Shannon

Website:

www.alphatrends.net

Email:

alphatrends@gmail.com

How long have you been active investing or trading in the financial markets?

1991

What year did you become active on Twitter?

2008

Services offered:

I wrote a book called "Technical Analysis Using Multiple Time frames" and I have a daily subscription service.

Which markets and instruments do you trade?

Individual stocks, ETFs, and Options.

Why did you choose these markets?

They chose me!

What type of trader do you consider yourself?

Swing Trader and Day Trader

Do you have a target for your average annual returns?

No

What time frame do you prefer to trade in, and do you ever change time frames?

2-5 days. I approach every trade as a potential swing trade, but if market action dictates, I day trade them.

What is the maximum drawdown you are willing to tolerate in pursuit of these returns?

It is more about focus on process than a number.

What technical indicators do you use to help quantify buy and sell signals?

Price, multiple time frames, VWAP and moving averages

Are there any chart patterns you use for trading?

Just the general cyclical nature of price action.

What was your best trading year and what did you learn?

Best percentage years were early on when I was fearless and didn't understand the importance of risk management. I was one of those traders who went all-in and got lucky with a trending market.

What was your worst trading year and what did you learn?

Worst, probably 1998 when the Nasdaq experienced a large pullback and I wasn't experienced enough to deal with it.

How do you quantify your entry into a trade? What parameters do you use?

Favorite setup is 1) Identify the trade on a daily time frame in the direction of the 50 and 200-day moving averages is where I identify the trade. 2) Determine potential risk vs reward on a 30-minute chart which covers approximately 45 days of data. I consider where it has come from and where it has the potential to go, as well as the personality of the stock for position sizing 3) I enter the trade after the stock has experienced a pullback/ consolidation and then resumes the previous, more powerful trend.

How do you manage your exit from a trade? What parameters do you use?

First, if it violates my stop I exit immediately. My stop is based on the most recent and relevant higher low in a long, for the time frame I am engaged. If the definition of trend, higher highs and higher lows no longer exists, so too does my reason to be involved. I also like to take partial profits on a quick spike. This allows me to reduce my risk quickly and then to raise the stop on the balance to a level where, if it's hit, the overall position doesn't lose money. When a position moves in my favor, I then try to raise my stop up under the most recent and relevant higher low for my time frame.

What is your favorite trading quote?

Only price pays!!

What are your favorite trading books?

Mine of course! Also, Stan Weinstein's, "Secrets for Profiting in Bull and Bear Markets". His work has had the biggest influence on how I view the markets. Anything by Brett Steenbarger. "How Charts Can Help You in the Stock Market" by Jiler, does a nice job of helping understand psychology of price patterns.

Who are your favorite traders to follow on Twitter?

http://alphatrends.net/archives/2015/12/21/top-twitter-traders-on-my-list/

Who has influenced you the most on your trading journey?

Early on as a broker at Lehman Brothers I was fortunate to work for a senior broker named Michael Collins. His focus on momentum really helped me recognize its importance.

What lessons have the markets taught you about yourself?

To be more patient. To be humble; being cocky is a quick way to go broke. To be more balanced in my trading and in my life.

What lessons have the markets taught you about other traders and investors?

Most people don't learn to think beyond their ego. They become emotionally attached to stocks and underestimate the importance of a strong defense.

What do you love about trading?

Being self-reliant and the continual intellectual challenge.

What do you find to be the most difficult aspect of trading?

That if we let our guard down, even the most experienced traders will repeat mistakes they know they shouldn't be making.

What are the biggest mistakes that lead to a trader's unprofitability?

Inexperienced traders are attracted to making big scores via options and the leveraged ETFs. You need to have a strong understanding of the cyclical flows of money as well as yourself before you try to size up.

What one piece of advice would you give to a new trader?

Go slow, the market will be here tomorrow. Focus on the process of making good trades and don't compare yourself to others.

@Alsabogal

Full time Equity/Option trader. Former head trader at $10bln HF. Swing/Channel trader using technical analysis to find attractive setups.

Name:

Al Sabogal

How long have you been active investing or trading in the financial markets?

25 years

What year did you become active on Twitter?

2010

Which markets and instruments do you trade?

Equities, options, and futures.

Why did you choose these markets?

Easy to understand and fit my comfort level.

What type of trader do you consider yourself?

Swing Trader

Do you have a target for your average annual returns?

No

What time frame do you prefer to trade in, and do you ever change time frames?

Swings can last from days to months. I rarely ever change time frames.

What is the maximum drawdown you are willing to tolerate in pursuit of these returns?

Depends on SPX.

What technical indicators do you use to help quantify buy and sell signals?

RSI, MACD, and moving averages.

Are there any chart patterns you use for trading?

Channels, bottoming plays, and breakouts.

What was your best trading year and what did you learn?

Best 2013 - The trend is your friend. Don't fight it.

What was your worst trading year and what did you learn?

Worst 2008 – Respect the power of a bear market and don't use leverage.

How do you quantify your entry into a trade? What parameters do you use?

Respecting a support level and seeing it move higher.

How do you manage your exit from a trade? What parameters do you use?

Reaching a resistance level along with near 70 RSI is usually a warning that risk/reward for staying long has deteriorated.

What is your favorite trading quote?

"The harder you work the luckier you get!" - Gary Player

What are your favorite trading books?

Market Wizards is the one that made me realize that trading is what I wanted to do with my life.

Who are your favorite traders to follow on Twitter?

@Canuck2usa, @Marketmodel, and @Ukarlewitz.

Who has influenced you the most on your trading journey?

So many different people it's hard to point to one or two. It's important to learn from everyone, good or bad, and take bits and pieces from those lessons to compliment your own style.

What lessons have the markets taught you about yourself?

The value of patience. Being patient and letting trends play out is a lot more powerful and profitable than trying to mastermind or micromanage moves.

What lessons have the markets taught you about other traders and investors?

Trading is road is long and full of curves on the way to success. It's a lot easier to be wrong than right, but so many want to pretend it's easy. Everyone wants to brag about winners, but you learn a lot more from the losing trades.

What do you love about trading?

The daily challenge that brings out conflicting emotions. The freedom to do it from anywhere in the world. The fact that a good trader never stops learning.

What do you find to be the most difficult aspect of trading?

Risk management. Many times it comes at a big cost, but it's an important tool to balance out fear and greed.

What are the biggest mistakes that lead to a trader's unprofitability?

Treating trading as gambling and not understanding proper risk management.

What one piece of advice would you give to a new trader?

Start with small money, because you will definitely be making mistakes during the learning process. It's the best education any trader gets, but how much it costs is up to you!

@Andrewnyquist

Founder of @seeitmarket. Active Investor. New Age Media. Sports Aficionado. Husband and Father of 3. Views are mine. RT's not endorsements.

Name:

Andy Nyquist

Website:

www.seeitmarket.com

Email:

andrew@seeitmarket.com

How long have you been active investing or trading in the financial markets?

16 years

What year did you become active on Twitter?

Which markets and instruments do you trade?

Equities (stocks, commodities, currencies, etc.)

Why did you choose these markets?

Equities are all I've traded, but ETFs allow for nuances of global capital flows and asset class shifts.

What type of trader do you consider yourself?

Swing Trader

Do you have a target for your average annual returns?

No

What time frame do you prefer to trade in, and do you ever change time frames?

Weeks. Anywhere from 3-6 weeks w/ trade around. When volatility emerges, time frames tighten and focused "days" trading used to preserve capital.

What is the maximum drawdown you are willing to tolerate in pursuit of these returns?

I focus mostly on ETFs, and as such I never want to lose more than 2 to 3 percent of my total capital on any focused trade. With stocks, it's tightened to roughly 1 percent.

What technical indicators do you use to help quantify buy and sell signals?

Relative Strength Index (trend, momentum and divergences), volume, price support, DeMark setups.

Are there any chart patterns you use for trading?

Retests, throwbacks, wedges, and rounded tops/bottoms.

What was your best trading year and what did you learn?

2009, 2010, and 2013 were the best.

What was your worst trading year and what did you learn?

2008 was the worst trading year (go figure). 2008 really ingrained the idea that cash is a position, and that precise short term opportunities exist on the short side.

How do you quantify your entry into a trade? What parameters do you use?

I always buy in "legs" to manage risk (i.e. 1/3, 1/3, 1/3). The idea is to make money and traders don't need to go all-in on their first purchase. Size matters.

How do you manage your exit from a trade? What parameters do you use?

I set a mental stop loss initially and move to a hard stop loss. I'll often lighten a position in "legs" just as I got in. A lighter position often keeps "emotions" out of a trade.

What is your favorite trading quote?

"Every day I assume every position I have is wrong." -Paul Tudor Jones

"At the end of the day, the most important thing is how good are you at risk control." -Paul Tudor Jones

What are your favorite trading books?

"Reminiscences of a Stock Operator" and "Market Wizards" books.

Who are your favorite traders to follow on Twitter?

@MarkArbeter, @CiovaccoCapital, @steenbab, and @BartsCharts

Who has influenced you the most on your trading journey?

My wife; she's been my best friend and my rock through it all. Can't beat that.

What lessons have the markets taught you about yourself?

That I am just as vulnerable to loss as the next trader, I have an undeniable strength to overcome adversity and learn from it. Finding an inner peace is key to maintaining a process and tuning out the noise (and emotion) that can bring traders/investors down.

What lessons have the markets taught you about other traders and investors?

It's a grind every day and you have to respect each other. Two traders may have a different opinion on a trade, but that difference is often due to time frames.

What do you love about trading?

Quantifying the risk associated with a trade setup and managing that risk in the trade.

What do you find to be the most difficult aspect of trading?

The waiting game. Sometimes there is a void in good setups and it's hard to sit still, but overtrading never leads to good things.

What are the biggest mistakes that lead to a trader's unprofitability?

Changing your trading thesis. Getting emotionally attached to a trade. Disrespecting your initial time frame. Overtrading.

What one piece of advice would you give to a new trader?

Scale into trades and set a stop. Small losses are a trader's best friend.

@Asennawealth

*Head Trader and founder of Asenna Wealth Solutions. Two top 10 finishes in the 07
and 08 CMC Trading Comps. 181% and 101% returns in 7 weeks using REAL money.*

Name:

Assad Tannous

Website:

www.asenna.com.au

Email:

Georgia@asenna.com.au

**How long have you been active investing or trading in the financial
markets?**

25 years

What year did you become active on Twitter?

2012

Services offered:

We offer SMS trade alerts, and if the client is interested, we place the trades and manage
the trade on their behalf.

Which markets and instruments do you trade?

We trade simple high probability pattern recognition across all markets.

What type of trader do you consider yourself?

Position Trader

Do you have a target for your average annual returns?

No

What time frame do you prefer to trade in, and do you ever change time frames?

Our time frame is dependent on the underlying instrument. We prefer to let winners ride and let the trailing stop take us out.

What is the maximum drawdown you are willing to tolerate in pursuit of these returns?

1%

What technical indicators do you use to help quantify buy and sell signals?

Trend lines, horizontal support, resistance, and price action. We look to catch major move breakouts and let positions ride. Looking to catch major moves makes holding winners easier.

Are there any chart patterns you use for trading?

Breakouts in the direction of the trend. For years I complicated trading until I finally realized that simple works. Simple also exerts the minimum amount of emotional capital and makes emotions easier to control.

What was your best trading year and what did you learn?

My best year was 1999 which was 480%, but that year I was coming off a very low base.

What was your worst trading year and what did you learn?
My worst year was 1997 which was -52%. I learned that I need to develop a strategy and system that had an edge.

How do you quantify your entry into a trade? What parameters do you use?
We use simple breakout recognition and we increase the probability on the break by only trading what I call 90% patterns. Sitting on the screen gives us a huge edge, as we have the luxury of watching PA and volume and entering before most other traders. It's not hard to tell where most traders will have alerts, so we tend to load up on the initial break and sell 1/2 into the first surge, reducing our average entry and eliminating whip on the retest.

How do you manage your exit from a trade? What parameters do you use?
We use trailing stops. There are exceptions; if a stock moves parabolic we will run the trailer just below the low of the previous daily bar. In theory, we end up selling the reversal bar on parabolic moves.

What is your favorite trading quote?
"Great traders understand the difference between looking for a trade and seeing the trade. Remain patient, they always come. When they do, it's obvious."

What are your favorite trading books?
"Reminiscences of a Stock Operator Market Wizard" series by Edwin Lefevre and "Trading in the Zone" by Mark Douglas.

Who are your favorite traders to follow on Twitter?
@David_Scutt, @ChrisWeston_IG, @SjosopehBurns, @Tradeciety, @Trader_Dante, @Trader_Mars, @Canuck2usa, and @Markminervini

Who has influenced you the most on your trading journey?
Jesse Livermore

What lessons have the markets taught you about yourself?
Patience is, always has been, and always will be the most underutilized trading tool.
There will always be other opportunities, don't force the trade. It's all about patience.

What lessons have the markets taught you about other traders and investors?
Most don't have any patience and feel like they always have to be trading.

What do you love about trading?
Trading will expose you like no other profession. The reason I did it is not because it's easy, but because it's hard. You owe it to yourself to be honest with yourself.

What do you find to be the hardest thing about trading?
I've been trading for 25 years and not trading is the only aspect of trading I continue to struggle with. The alternative is to lose money and trading without an edge. It must be done.

What are the biggest mistakes that lead to a trader's unprofitability?
Lack of patience and overtrading. It's as simple as that. Most traders are so obsessed with the short term moves that they fail to see the big moves when they play out. By the time they realize it's a big move, it's usually to complain about selling too early.

What one piece of advice would you give to a new trader?
Find another job.

@Canuck2usa2

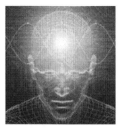

*Disclaimer: Trades/charts or my setups are for informational purposes only & not a recommendation to buy or sell securities of any kind *Trade at your Own Risk**

Website:

www.Cthelighttrading.com

Email:

Cthelighttrading@gmail.com

How long have you been active investing or trading in the financial markets?

25 years

What year did you become active on Twitter?

2014

Services offered:

Educational Website along with Alerts and Position management for Common Stock/Options and Futures.

Which markets and instruments do you trade?
Futures common stock and options.

Why did you choose these markets?
Futures for leverage and around the clock availability, Common for longer term horizon with no decay or expiry, and options for leverage.

What type of trader do you consider yourself?
Momentum Trader, Swing Trader, and Trend Follower.

Do you have a target for your average annual returns?
Yes

What time frame do you prefer to trade in, and do you ever change time frames?
I prefer to use multiple timeframes to analyze.

What is the maximum drawdown you are willing to tolerate in pursuit of these returns?
10%

What technical indicators do you use to help quantify buy and sell signals?
Elliot Wave, moving averages, trend lines, and momentum indicators.

Are there any chart patterns you use for trading?
Ending diagonals and flags

What were your best and worst trading years and what did you learn from them?

Best years- 2007-08

Worst years- 1987 2001

Be prepared to stay in a position longer than you expect and when wrong, exit as quickly as possible.

How do you quantify your entry into a trade? What parameters do you use?

Fibs along with location within a set pattern based on Elliot Wave theory

How do you manage your exit from a trade? What parameters do you use?

Support levels along with fibs and location within a pattern based on Elliot Wave and extensions for my targets.

What is your favorite trading quote?

"I believe the very best money is made at the market turns. Everyone says you get killed trying to pick tops and bottoms and you make all your money by playing the trend in the middle. Well for 12 years I have been missing the meat in the middle but I have made a lot of money at tops and bottoms." -Paul Tudor Jones

What are your favorite trading books?

"Elliot Wave Principle", "Mental Game of Poker", "Technical Analysis of Financial Markets".

Who are you favorite traders to follow on Twitter?

Steve Burns and MasterTrader.

Who has influenced you the most on your trading journey?

My Mentor.

What lessons have the markets taught you about yourself?
It's a game of self-control.

What lessons have the markets taught you about other traders and investors?
That the winners are systematic and controlled, while the losers are the opposite and gamble and trade with emotion.

What do you love about trading?
Freedom. No boss.

What do you find to be the toughest thing about trading?
Risk control.

What do you believe are the biggest mistakes that traders make that lead to unprofitability?
Stray from their system and trade on hope.

What one piece of advice would you give to a new trader?
Read and practice for already 1-2 years.

@CiovaccoCapital

CEO: Voted "Most Helpful" To Investors on Twitter. Use proprietary model to manage accounts for individual investors. How can model help you? See CCM website.

Name:

Chris Ciovacco

Website:

www.ciovaccocapital.com

How long have you been active investing or trading in the financial markets?

Since 1994

What year did you become active on Twitter?

March 2011

Services offered:

We have taken concepts used successfully by top traders for years, and adjusted them to an investor's time frame. Our firm uses a proprietary and rules-based asset allocation model to manage client accounts on a discretionary basis.

Which markets and instruments do you trade?

We use ETFs to invest in U.S. stocks, sectors, regions of the globe, individual countries, bonds, oil, gold, silver, copper, currencies, etc.

Why did you choose these markets?

Stocks and bonds are not the only options for investors. Under certain conditions, other asset classes can offer a better risk-reward profile for investors. For example, during a period between October 2001 and July 2008, a diversified basket of commodities gained over 150%; over the same period the S&P 500 gained less than 15%. Over-weighting defensive assets in bear markets can also add significant value for investors. During the financial crisis, long-term Treasury bonds were up over 40% in December 2008; over the same period the S&P 500 was down over 40%. Methods used by successful traders can help investors as well.

What type of trader do you consider yourself?

Trend Follower

Do you have a target for your average annual returns?

No

What time frame do you prefer to trade in, and do you ever change time frames?

Our asset allocation model uses data and charts on daily, weekly, and monthly time frames. Most investors focus on one time frame, but using multiple time frames can significantly increase our odds of success.

What is the maximum drawdown you are willing to tolerate in pursuit of these returns?

Prefer maximum draw to stay near 8% to 11% range.

What technical indicators do you use to help quantify buy and sell signals?

Too many to list, but here are a few: Moving averages, MACD, RSI, CCI, Coppock Curve, ROC, Stochastics, and Williams %R.

Are there any chart patterns you use for trading?

Our model doesn't use chart patterns, however, we do use them as part of the implementation rules; head-and-shoulders, cup-and-handles, and trend channels.

What was your best and worst trading year and what did you learn?

In 2008, charts and facts were very helpful. 2011 reinforced the concept of "we do not know what is going to happen next". The S&P 500 had a very bearish profile in early October 2011. After the ECB hinted at providing assistance to European banks, the S&P 500 flipped from risk-off to risk-on very quickly. The ECB eventually offered unlimited three-year loans to banks. I will never forget seeing the S&P 500's 50-day start to turn back up in October 2011 and thinking "this doesn't fit the bear market profile". Charts can't predict the future; they can only help us with probabilities. When the "knowns" or facts change, the market adjusts to the new information. We must be willing to adjust as well, and do it very quickly under rare and higher-risk circumstances.

How do you quantify your entry into a trade? What parameters do you use?

Our master market model tells us a prudent allocation between risk assets such as stocks, and conservative assets such as bonds. We also have a rules and data-based ETF scoring system. Both models govern our entries and exits, including the magnitude of the shift (position sizing).

How do you manage your exit from a trade? What parameters do you use?

Our model helps us discern between "volatility to ignore", meaning hold our position, and "volatility to respect", meaning it's time to book profits or reduce risk. It's all based on facts and rules. Opinions, forecasting, and emotions have no place in our system.

What is your favorite trading quote?

"Markets set asset prices, rather than personal opinions."

What are your favorite trading books?

Covel's Trend-Following helps give us the belief that "it can be done". My favorite story is the one about the trend follower who was so successful he was able to buy the Boston Red Sox. His name John W. Henry. The first step to becoming successful at anything is having an unwavering belief that "it can be done". Despite the skepticism about technical analysis, I have zero doubt in my mind that it can be done. I am confident the other traders in this book feel the same way.

Who are your favorite traders to follow on Twitter?

We don't spend a lot of time on the feeds of other traders for two reasons: (1) we are confident in our system, and more importantly (2) a big part of our system is based on making decisions based on facts. The only way to do that is to remain as unbiased as humanly possible. Having said that, we always enjoy and respect the work of @SJosephBurns, @RyanDetrick, @RedDogT3, @Traderstewie, @Jboorman,

@Canuck2usa, @SharpTraders, @Alsabogal, just to name a few. Twitter has some very competent traders that are generous with their time and talents. We can all learn from each other; no one has a monopoly on all the good ideas.

Who has influenced you the most on your trading journey?

Reading books like this one gives us exposure to successful traders. Success is not easy in this business. Our approach has been influenced by the success stories of many, including those profiled in The Market Wizards. However, the biggest influence has been the market. The best way to learn about the markets is to study the markets. It doesn't matter how we think things should work, all that matters are how markets actually work. Markets set asset prices. Markets determine if our allocations make money.

What lessons have the markets taught you about yourself?

Markets eventually teach us all the same lessons. We are all human. Humans have an intense desire to be right, which is tied to our ego. Over time we all learn this is not about being right or being a great forecaster, but rather the purpose is to prudently grow and preserve our hard-earned capital. My guess is every trader in this book has something in common; we all have made mistakes, we all got tired of making mistakes, we all studied the markets and developed some form of discipline and structure that reduces the probability of making the same mistakes, which in turn greatly increases our probability of producing successful outcomes over the long-term.

What lessons have the markets taught you about other traders and investors?

Experience counts. The difference between a successful trader and a new trader is the successful trader has learned from their mistakes. We all make mistakes in the beginning; it is how we evolve and learn.

What do you love about trading?

Markets are based on economics, human psychology, and math; three things that I enjoy. Markets are incredibly difficult and challenging. Most people enjoy being challenged; it is why we play sports/cards/chess, go to trivia night, or sit down with a crossword puzzle.

What do you find to be the hardest thing about trading?

Markets can be highly frustrating at times. The key is to remember the markets never single us out. Markets are difficult for everyone. 2015 was the worst year for asset allocation managers since 1938. It was not an easy year for anyone.

What are the biggest mistakes that lead to a trader's unprofitability?

Trading based on emotion, breaking rules, and staying too close to volatility. Stress accumulates over time in the markets. It is important to get away regularly. We exercise and make sure we get away from the PCs and cell phones from time-to-time.

What one piece of advice would you give to a new trader?

A very small percentage of traders "make it". If you have an intense desire to be successful and are willing to study, learn from others, and correct mistakes, you can make it too. You're human which means you can learn a lot about markets by simply observing your own behavior and emotions.

@EdMatts

Senior Technical Strategist at Capital Management. Combining 20+ years' experience of trading, economics and politics.

Name:

Ed Matts

Website:

www.Marketvisiontv.com

Email:

edmattsX@gmail.com

How long have you been active investing or trading in the financial markets?

From the time I was a teenager, 30+ years.

What year did you become active on Twitter?

Services offered:

Profit-oriented evidenced based (mainly technical) analysis on currencies indices and commodities.

Which markets and instruments do you trade?

Most. Indices/stocks/bonds/currencies/Ems.

Why did you choose these markets?

They chose me.

What type of trader do you consider yourself?

Momentum Trader, Swing Trader, Trend Follower, Day Trader, Position Trader, and more.

Do you have a target for your average annual returns?

Yes

What time frame do you prefer to trade in, and do you ever change time frames?

Wherever there is most 'volaclarity' = Volatility and Clarity. Minutes to years.

What is the maximum drawdown you are willing to tolerate in pursuit of these returns?

Mainly 1%. Sometimes 4% for the big plays, i.e. Gold 10% recently.

What technical indicators do you use to help quantify buy and sell signals?

Whatever indicator is working or to the fore. But the closest to reality in my opinion. Elliott Wave / Fractals /evidenced based traditional analysis.

Are there any chart patterns you use for trading?

All of them

What was your best and worst trading year and what did you learn?

1998. A view is not necessarily a trade.

How do you quantify your entry into a trade? What parameters do you use?

Price action /sentiment and, importantly, Risk Return x Probability.

How do you manage your exit from a trade? What parameters do you use?

In multiples relating to the change in risk/return probability. I don't try to squeeze all the pips out of the market.

What is your favorite trading quote?

"You may think you are in the business of trading. But you are in the business of decision making. And the better you can make these decisions ahead of time, the better your result will be." - Paul Tudor Jones

What are your favorite trading books?

"Reminiscences of a Stock Operator" (with Paul Tudor Jones foreword) by Jesse Livermore

Who are your favorite traders to follow on Twitter?

Myself or everyone. Seek lots of advice but keep your own counsel.

Who has influenced you the most on your trading journey?

My wife and children, so that I don't put them at risk but instead maximize their wealth and happiness.

What lessons have the markets taught you about yourself?

However good your results may be, never have an ego. Always seek to improve. Be passionate in your analysis but disciplined in your execution.

What lessons have the markets taught you about other traders and investors?

They are greedy, fearful, and callous as a crowd. But as individuals they are fun, clever, and need protecting.

What do you love about trading?

Everything. Trading is a very intense representation of life. Rigorous intellectual pursuit, immense highs, sometimes big lows, and doubt. But always hope and a strong sense of self-preservation.

What do you find to be the most difficult aspect of trading?

Leaving it alone and taking a break.

What are the biggest mistakes that lead to a trader's unprofitability?

There are many clichéd reasons for losses or failure, like letting losses run or taking profits too early. Most reasons stem from emotion. Therefore, it's important to have the ability to step back and see what is going on in the market and with yourself.

What one piece of advice would you give to a new trader?

Lose. If you can learn the lessons of losses early without too much cost or pain, then it will put you in very good stead for an entire trading career.

@Ew_trader

I use Elliot Wave to determine trade set ups. My tweets are for information only. It should not be taken as trading advice.

How long have you been active investing or trading in the financial markets?

10 years

What year did you become active on Twitter?

2014

Which markets and instruments do you trade?

Only trade ASX200 Index, German DAX index, and S&P 500 index.

Why did you choose these markets?

German DAX - volatility, ASX 200 - local index and S&P 500 - most traded index.

What type of trader do you consider yourself?

Day Trader

Do you have a target for your average annual returns?

No

What time frame do you prefer to trade in, and do you ever change time frames?

I would like to become a swing trader and do day trades on the side, but haven't managed to be patient with a swing position yet.

What is the maximum drawdown you are willing to tolerate in pursuit of these returns?

10% capital

What technical indicators do you use to help quantify buy and sell signals?

I primarily use Elliot Waves calculations for day trades and use Gann cycle timing to try and setup swing positions. I also look at MACD, RSI, and Bollinger Bands to support EW calculations.

Are there any chart patterns you use for trading?

I am familiar with head and shoulders and inverse head and shoulders. I find EW to be the most accurate to set up trades.

What was your best trading year and what did you learn?

Best years were 2005, 2006, and 2007.

What was your worst trading year and what did you learn?

Worst trading years were 2008 and 2009. Learned EW and Gann timing because of it. Prior to that I used SMAs and Bollinger Bands to trade.

How do you quantify your entry into a trade? What parameters do you use?

I use EW calculations and Fib levels to determine entry. I place stop at 50% of the range between one Fib level and the next one. I also do separate EW calcs on RTH data and futures data to find areas of alignment.

How do you manage your exit from a trade? What parameters do you use?

I exit based on EW calculations as well. I don't have any specific parameters that I use.

What is your favorite trading quote?

I don't have one. But if I did, it would be: *"Keep your losses small and let your winners run."*

What are your favorite trading books?

Elliot Wave principles

Who are your favorite traders to follow on Twitter?

@Jim8080, @Hubon, @Marketrend, and @Sagaron62.

Who has influenced you the most on your trading journey?

Bill McLaren

What lessons have the markets taught you about yourself?

I am not a patient or disciplined person and until I learn to be both, I can't get the best out of the market.

What lessons have the markets taught you about other traders and investors?

"The market is a mechanism to transfer money from the impatient to the patient." – Warren Buffet. I find that the best traders are those that are humble and helpful and have a sense of humor.

What do you love about trading?

I love doing the analysis and EW calculations, especially when they come off. After joining Twitter, I also love to help other traders and often share my thought process with them.

What do you find to be the most difficult aspect of trading?

Being patient and sticking to a plan, especially when things don't go as I expected.

What are the biggest mistakes that lead to a trader's unprofitability?

Failing to close a losing position quickly and hoping it comes back due to an inability to take a loss. Trading against the trend. Failing to hold a position to target by closing too early.

What one piece of advice would you give to a new trader?

Learn as much as you can about the market before putting real money to work. Follow some successful traders and practice on a demo account. Be clear about entry and exit rules and always stick to those rules.

Ivanhoff

Founder of http://SocialLeverage50.com, Author of The 5 Secrets To Highly Profitable Swing Trading and a few other books: http://www.amazon.com/Ivaylo-Ivanov/e/B00O1Z5OYM, full-time trader.

Name:

Ivan Hoff

Website:

www.ivanhoff.com

Email:

ivaylo.ivanoff@gmail.com

How long have you been active investing or trading in the financial markets?

12 years

What year did you become active on Twitter?

2008

Services offered:

www.SocialLeverage50.com

Which markets and instruments do you trade?

U.S. stocks

Why did you choose these markets?

Very liquid, providing plenty of opportunities every week.

What type of trader do you consider yourself?

Swing Trader

Do you have a target for your average annual returns?

Yes

What time frame do you prefer to trade in, and do you ever change time frames?

I usually trade on a daily time frame, unless the market becomes super-volatile as in during corrections. Then, I drill down to 5-minute charts.

What is the maximum drawdown you are willing to tolerate in pursuit of these returns?

What technical indicators do you use to help quantify buy and sell signals?

Momentum, 5, 10, and 20-day moving averages.

Are there any chart patterns you use for trading?

Bull flags and wedges, flat bases.

What was your best trading year and what did you learn?

Best was 2013 - when the market environment is favorable for your market approach, make sure that you trade aggressively and take full advantage of it.

What was your worst trading year and what did you learn?

Worst was 2008 - the goal in a bear market is to survive whole, not to swing for the fences.

How do you quantify your entry into a trade? What parameters do you use?

I am looking for a momentum pivot. On the long side, it is 10-20 cents above previous resistance. Depending on the market and the setup, sometimes I'll enter in an anticipation of a breakout or breakdown.

How do you manage your exit from a trade? What parameters do you use?

I use partial exits:

Sell 1/3 to 1/2 when you are up the amount at risk. For example, if I buy a stock at 20 with a stop at 19, I'd sell 1/3 to 1/2 when it reaches 21. Sell the rest 3 to 10 days after the trigger. Most stocks move in momentum bursts of 3 to 10 days. Then they enter into trendless consolidation through time or mean-revert.

What is your favorite trading quote?

"Momentum investing is a contrarian approach."

What are your favorite trading books?

"Hedge Fund Market Wizards" by Jack Schwager, "Superperformance Stocks" by Richard Love, and "Trading in the Zone" by Mark Douglas.

Who are your favorite traders to follow on Twitter?

@Howardlindzon, @Zortrades, @Jfahmy, @Alphatrends, and @Steenbab

Who has influenced you the most on your trading journey?

My trading diary, which I diligently fill out every day.

What lessons have the markets taught you about yourself?

Never say never. Don't trade when you are out of sync with the market. Better to take a break and come back with a fresh perspective. If I deliberately work on improving my strengths, I get a lot better over time.

What lessons have the markets taught you about other traders and investors?

People rarely change.

What do you love about trading?

It is an intellectual and psychological challenge that keeps you on your toes every day. Nothing better.

What do you find to be the most difficult aspect of trading?

The waiting. Trading requires extreme patience.

What are the biggest mistakes that lead to a trader's unprofitability?

They don't cut losses short, don't position size properly, trade methods that don't work in current specific market environment, and use too much leverage.

What one piece of advice would you give to a new trader?

Learn how to consistently make money with one setups first. Then, start adding additional setups to your portfolio.

@JBoorman

Trend Follower, Portfolio Manager, Chartered Market Technician. Manage money @BroadswordCap. Blog / Premium at Alpha Capture. Frontman for @StrangeBrewNC.

Name:

Jon Boorman

Website:

www.jonboorman.com

How long have you been active investing or trading in the financial markets?

I've worked in financial markets in various roles since 1987.

What year did you become active on Twitter?

2013

Services offered:

My blog is Alpha Capture at jonboorman.com and I'm also a Registered Investment Adviser at Broadsword Capital where I manage client money.

Which markets and instruments do you trade?

U.S. stocks

Why did you choose these markets?

As I moved towards managing client money and being regulated, it became more important to specialize in one area.

What type of trader do you consider yourself?

Trend Follower

Do you have a target for your average annual returns?

I don't target a specific return each year but I aim for absolute returns and expect to beat the market over time.

What time frame do you prefer to trade in, and do you ever change time frames?

I typically hold positions weeks to months. I don't change time frames, but in a strong bull market I will have signals via all-time highs or 52-week highs. After a prolonged market downturn, my entries may come from 50-day or multi-month highs.

What is the maximum drawdown you are willing to tolerate in pursuit of these returns?

I would be concerned about the viability of a system once the drawdown exceeded 3x its expected annual return.

What technical indicators do you use to help quantify buy and sell signals?

Price is the lead, moving averages are the supporting cast, and volume, relative strength, and ATR are co-stars.

Are there any chart patterns you use for trading?

I don't trade the patterns themselves as many have specific price targets (which I don't use). However, I will often recognize 'ascending triangles' 'flags/pennants' or 'cup and handle' patterns when I'm taking an entry as a simple breakout to new highs.

What was your best trading year and what did you learn?

Possibly guilty of some recency bias here, but I think 2013 will stand out for a long time as a great year for anyone following trends on stocks. 2003/04 as a prop trader at Lehman sowed the seeds for much of what I am today as a trader.

What was your worst year as a trader and what did you learn?

2015 was a very tough environment for my time frame, with severe drops that were met with equally sharp rallies. Going back further, the 1987 crash gave me my first brutal lesson on margin.

How do you quantify your entry into a trade? What parameters do you use?

I want to have reward/risk of at least two to one, ideally three. That doesn't mean it's a price target, but if the stock is a utility and I'm risking 0.5% of my account with a stop 10% away, then realistically with all other things considered, is it going to go up 20% or 30% for me to make 1-1.5%? Maybe, but if the same chart setup were on an IBD name that's probably going to have more appeal in a strong market. Not all stocks trade alike. This is where ATR can be used to good effect too, for stops and position sizing.

How do you manage your exit from a trade? What parameters do you use?

If you have a rationale when you enter a trade, your exit should simply be an invalidation of that. Place your stop where you're wrong, that way you won't hesitate to honor it when it hits. I exit when the stock is no longer in an uptrend for my time frame.

What is your favorite trading quote?

"Observe that the blade of grass that resists the lawnmower gets cut down, while the blade that bends remains uncut." - Paul Tudor Jones

What are your favorite trading books?

"Reminiscences of a Stock Operator" by Lefevre, all the Schwager Market Wizards books, and all titles by Michael Covel, Van Tharp, Andreas Clenow.

Who are your favorite traders to follow on Twitter?

Too many to list! Look at who I follow. It's taken 3 years to cultivate that list of over 500.

Who has influenced you the most on your trading journey?

Mr. Market. The tuition is expensive but the lessons stay with you. He's an excellent teacher.

What lessons have the markets taught you about yourself?

Through trial and error and over many years, I have arrived at a mindset and methodology that suits who I am as a person and as a trader. The market has taught me who I am, what I can and cannot do, and what I can and cannot control.

What lessons have the markets taught you about other traders and investors?

That just as you will meet every type of character and person in life, you will also meet them in the market. It's all just people.

What do you love about trading?

It has taught me who I am, and what I believe about markets. It's a means by which you can build wealth, but it's also unpredictable. It's a stimulating and never-ending challenge, emotionally and psychologically.

What do you find to be the most difficult aspect of trading?

That as humans we're not wired to succeed at it. You literally have to learn to go against your strongest natural instincts in order to do well.

What are the biggest mistakes that lead to a trader's unprofitability?

They concentrate too much on finding entries and how much they can make rather than what they could lose. Many are also unaware of the impact of position sizing or how to do it correctly.

What one piece of advice would you give to a new trader?

Read as much as you can. Learn from those who have succeeded. But most of all, be patient. The market will always be there.

@JustinPulitzer

'Do or do not. There is no try.' -Yoda, Jedi Master. Prop Trader blending Technicals, Fundamentals & Macro. NYU Stern Business Alum. #PriceIsTruth #Lower4Longer

Name:

Justin Pulitzer

YouTube channel:

https://m.youtube.com/c/JustinPulitzerTrades

How long have you been active investing or trading in the financial markets?

Since I was a kid. I had a trading account at 18.

What year did you become active on Twitter?

2009

Services offered:

I will eventually launch a paid subscription service, but I currently post free trade ideas, commentary, weekend review YouTube videos and Periscope Live Q & A sessions.

Which markets and instruments do you trade?

I trade in the leading momentum issues like: SPY, QQQ, IWM, AAPL, FB, AMZN, NFLX, GOOGL, TSLA, PCLN etc.

Why did you choose these markets?

Liquidity and predictable option premium IV.

What type of trader do you consider yourself?

Momentum Trader, Swing Trader, Trend Follower, Day Trader, Position Trader

Do you have a target for your average annual returns?

No

What time frame do you prefer to trade in, and do you ever change time frames?

I tend to stay inside of 30 days maximum, but often do spreads and ratios in same or next week options series.

What is the maximum drawdown you are willing to tolerate in pursuit of these returns?

10% max...15% if I get blindsided and then I go flat.

What technical indicators do you use to help quantify buy and sell signals?

Reference horizontal supports and resistance levels, Trend lines, Fibonacci retracements and extensions (61.8 and 1.618), and Stochastic Momentum Index.

Are there any chart patterns you use for trading?

I like the head and shoulders and inverse head and shoulders patterns. They're very visual and often become self-fulfilling prophesies. Playing for the initial breakdown isn't always the easy money, but a failed check-back to the neckline is usually great.

What was your worst trading year and what did you learn?

2008-2009 were not good. I was just getting into trading full-time and was a great puncher, but didn't know how to block yet---lesson learned. Rick Management is quite possibly the most important skill a trader can acquire. I did a Risk Management 101 Video that's on my YouTube channel. I suggest watching it.

How do you quantify your entry into a trade? What parameters do you use?

I tend to like risking 1 to make 3. Sometimes I'll do 1 for 2, but tend to be very conservative. I don't like moonshots, but prefer to play for the surer money. Gamblers play for long-shot jackpots, professionals play to win.

How do you manage your exit from a trade? What parameters do you use?

I like to take profits along the way at predetermined targets with the previously mentioned technical indicators. If for any reason I no longer believe my setup is valid, I get out. A common mistake is allowing your existing position to determine your bias when it should be the opposite. Position should be determined by bias.

What is your favorite trading quote?

"They say there are two sides to everything. But there is only one side to the stock market; and it is not the bull side or the bear side, but the right side." - Jesse Livermore

"Emotional control is the most essential factor in playing the market. Never lose control of your emotions when the market moves against you. Don't get too confident over your wins or too despondent over your losses." - Jesse Livermore

What are your favorite trading books?

"Reminiscences of a Stock Operator" by Edwin Lefevre and "How to Trade in Stocks" by Jesse Livermore.

Who are your favorite traders to follow on Twitter?

I honestly don't pay much attention to other traders. I find their work and bias can influence my own, and that usually leads me to second guessing my own work. 9 times out of 10 I regret not just following my own work. It's usually correct.

Who has influenced you the most on your trading journey?

Jesse Livermore

What lessons have the markets taught you about yourself?

The markets teach humility on a daily basis. Don't hesitate or second guess yourself. Believe it or not, your gut is usually correct. Trust yourself and make the tough decisions quickly before it's too late.

What lessons have the markets taught you about other traders and investors?

Too often in life, we worry about what other people think about us. How we stack up to other people. The truth is they aren't your competition, you are. You just have to be your best self. Don't worry about what others are doing or say they're doing. Just keep your eye on the prize, your own P & L.

What do you love about trading?

I like not having to deal with people. In most businesses you have to deal with office politics and incompetence. In trading you can make money on the very incompetence that would frustrate you in any other circumstance outside of the stock market.

What do you find to be the most difficult aspect of trading?

Patience. Winning setups often take time to play out. Watching the market all day can get boring and tempting to over trade. It's impossible to catch every move in every stock, every day. It's hard to see a stock up or down big and not be in it, but that is part of the discipline. Over trading is very costly.

What are the biggest mistakes that lead to a trader's unprofitability?

They're hopeful when they should be fearful and fearful when they should be hopeful. For example, you're right in a trade and the stock is moving your direction, but you get nervous about losing a profit and book profits too soon, and of course the stock never looks back from there. On the other hand, being in a losing position and making excuses for it and hoping it "comes back."

What one piece of advice would you give to a new trader?

Keep your size small and manage risk. Using too much leverage will destroy you. When things are going well, it's amazing. But the geometric series swings both ways and markets usually move downward faster than upward.

@Mella_TA

International pain in the Ass. Lover of Global Markets. $SPX sniper. Wife of The Northman @NorthmanTrader Visit http://mellatrades.com.

Website:

http://mellatrades.com

Email:

mellatrades@gmail.com

How long have you been active investing or trading in the financial markets?

since 2009

What year did you become active on Twitter?

2011

Services offered:

Technical and market analysis.

Which markets and instruments do you trade?

US and Europe global indices. Gold, oil and banks

Why did you choose these markets?

Because I know how they tick.

What type of trader do you consider yourself?

Momentum Trader, Swing Trader, and Position Trader

Do you have a target for your average annual returns?

Yes

What time frame do you prefer to trade in, and do you ever change time frames?

Daily, 4-hour, and weekly.

What is the maximum drawdown you are willing to tolerate in pursuit of these returns?

8%

What technical indicators do you use to help quantify buy and sell signals?

My proprietary signals.

Are there any chart patterns you use for trading?

I use many. Flags, inverses, wedges etc.

What was your best trading year and what did you learn?

2010 was a great year for me as I was first introduced to the markets after the crash. I found great value in many companies so I bought and held. 2014 became my best year as I finally worked out the best dynamics of really trading these markets.

How do you quantify your entry into a trade? What parameters do you use?

I scale in or I use a wider stop.

How do you manage your exit from a trade? What parameters do you use?

I scale out and have targets.

What is your favorite trading quote?

"This is a dirty business but somebody has to do it."

What are your favorite trading books?

None

Who are your favorite traders to follow on Twitter?

I follow SpongeBob, sorry!

Who has influenced you the most on your trading journey?

The trolls and so called professionals on Twitter. Both are useless and made me seek and perfect my own craft #KISS

What lessons have the markets taught you about yourself?

That risk management is key and that the battle is with yourself as a trader and not the markets. If you can master risk and emotions, you will succeed.

What lessons have the markets taught you about other traders and investors?

Crowd behavior; most are extremely fearful at the bottom and totally giddy at the top.

What do you love about trading?

I love the thrill of solving the complex puzzle of these markets. Finding and timing the direction, executing trades gladiator-style, and banking big.

What do you find to be the most difficult aspect of trading?

Staying focused on my own findings and not being distracted by news or other people's opinions.

What are the biggest mistakes that lead to a trader's unprofitability?

Over exposure and emotions.

What one piece of advice would you give to a new trader?

Stay patient and build slowly. Trading is not a race. Safe, steady gains are a must.

@Northmantrader

Futures & options trader, entrepreneur, serial expat. Keeping it real, but light. For market analysis or to join our trading community please visit the site.

Website:

www.northmantrader.com

How long have you been active investing or trading in the financial markets?

18 years

What year did you become active on Twitter?

2012

Services offered:

We operate a trading community which gives members access to our directional calls based on our technical charts, trade process, risk management, and market analysis.

Which markets and instruments do you trade?

U.S. and global indices and commodities, with emphasis on $ES and $DAX. Primary trading vehicles are futures and option markets.

Why did you choose these markets?

Futures in particular offer round the clock trading at low commissions and precise stop management. This combination permits traders to partake in directional opportunities that avail themselves outside of standard U.S. market hours.

What type of trader do you consider yourself?

Swing Trader and Day Trader

Do you have a target for your average annual returns?

Yes

What time frame do you prefer to trade in, and do you ever change time frames?

I'm flexible in regards to time frames and will adapt according to market conditions. Most trade setups may last a day to a week, swing trades may last several weeks.

What is the maximum drawdown you are willing to tolerate in pursuit of these returns?

Option trades are usually limited to 1-3% of capital. Future trades are risk managed via a stop management process that usually limits drawdown to a predetermined amount of handles.

What technical indicators do you use to help quantify buy and sell signals?

On the signal front I prefer $BPSPX, $NYAD, $NYMO, $NYSI, $TICK, etc. Some of the most profitable setups are found in analyzing charts in context of structures, divergences, trend lines, gaps, and price magnets. To this end, standard charting tools such as RSIs, MACDs, Fib levels, etc. Select moving averages on multiple time frames can be of great use.

Are there any chart patterns you use for trading?

I'm always keeping my eye on potential emerging patterns and defining levels at which potential patterns either trigger or invalidate. The key is to know when the pattern no longer applies. Standard pattern of interest are bull/bear flags, standard or inverse heads and shoulders patterns, wedges of all sorts, cup and handles, etc.

What was your best and worst trading year and what did you learn?

Ironically, the best trading years can be the worst and vice versa, and the reason is psychology. Early in my trading career, I had a tremendous year trading options. It got to the point that it seemed almost *too* easy. The predictable danger, a sense of invincibility crept in and I increased exposure. What can go wrong, right? Well, everything. Once a trader is too exposed, a gap move can do a lot of damage to an account. Not only that, but losses tend to invite revenge trading; trying to make up losses. This is not a positive mindset to be in when trading and probably a lesson that most traders experience at one point or another. Measured exposure and stop management are important elements of account management, keeping leakage to a minimum. My best trading years have come as a result of incorporating these lessons into a trading process that I can repeatedly apply and execute on. If a trade goes against me, I know ahead of time what my risk exposure is, and this keeps my psychology and emotions in check.

How do you quantify your entry into a trade? What parameters do you use?

Charts, technical and market analysis help inform trade direction and entry levels I am interested in pursuing. They're a compass that help me identify where I want to go. However, the character of the tape action dictates how aggressive or measured I want to pursue a certain entry. For example, in extremely volatile market conditions, I may use much smaller exposure, but wider stops, whereas in lower volatility environments I may have a greater level of comfort with exposure. Getting a feel for the tape is not something learned overnight. It takes years and probably evolves into a sixth sense for experienced traders.

How do you manage your exit from a trade? What parameters do you use?

I scale out usually in steps of 20% from the original positions. The rationale is simple: My job is to generate gains on a consistent basis as possible. And no matter how good a technical setup may be, I can't be sure targets will be fully reached. So I keep myself honest by scaling out of a position as key levels are reached. Once the first scale out is taken and the trade is profitable, adjusting stops along the way helps keep it that way. So if a setup fails to follow through or breaks apart you still have a profitable trade. It also helps prevent stubbornness or being fixated on a particular setup. Flexibility is key.

What is your favorite trading quote?

Don't know if it's a trading quote but here's my mantra: *"If a position keeps you awake at night, it's too big or not risk defined!"*

What are your favorite trading books?

This may surprise, but I've never read a trading book in my life. I'm completely self-taught and have the emotional scars to prove it.

Who are your favorite traders to follow on Twitter?

@Mella_TA, @SlopeOfHope, and @SJosephBurns

Who has influenced you the most on your trading journey?

My wife Mella_TA. She's the best chartist I know with an ungodly patience to wait for the right setups. Most impressive to me, her targets always get hit.

What lessons have the markets taught you about yourself?

If you want to be a consistently good trader check your ego at the door. It's more important to make money than to be right. A college professor of mine once told me that wisdom is the art of knowing what to ignore, and this is certainly true when it comes to trading. As someone who has a keen interest in the details of how the world works, I've found myself getting too caught up in the noise that's the markets. One needs to be able to either step away or emotionally distance oneself emotionally. For example, as a trader, it serves no purpose to argue central bank policy, the pros and cons of HFTs, politics, economics, etc. It's all interesting and it's good to be informed, but at the end of the day, none of it tells you what is a good level to buy or when to exit a trade.

What lessons have the markets taught you about other traders and investors?

At its most simplistic: People get bullish at tops and bearish at bottoms. Getting good data and a solid feel of sentiment can help inform your trade direction, either as a contrarian trader or a momentum follower. However, while the crowd is eventually almost always wrong, the crowd can also be right for quite a while, and it's hard to fade a crowd when it's running you over ;-). When people want tulips they want tulips. Until they don't. And when they want to run toward an exit, know when the rush is ebbing before you get in the way.

What do you love about trading?

It gives me complete control over my life because it gives me scalability in income that a salaried person otherwise could not achieve. I can choose to trade or not trade, and I can do it from where ever I choose. I'm not locked into a particular location. Hence I love the flexibility. I also love the puzzle. Being presented with ever changing market conditions and complex variables is an enormous intellectual challenge and I thrive on that challenge.

What do you find to be the most difficult aspect of trading?

The influence of HFTs and computerized trading can gnaw on the psychology of any trader. More often than not we can observe 'fake' moves or 'rumors' that can take one out of otherwise perfectly good setups. This environment probably makes trading more difficult than it needs to be, but it is the environment we have and we must adapt.

What are the biggest mistakes that lead to a trader's unprofitability?

Too much exposure, not defining risk, no stops, no trade process or plan, revenge trading, over trading, and being too emotionally involved.

What one piece of advice would you give to a new trader?

Understand how psychology can impact your trading. If you feel anxious, step away and analyze what's driving the emotion. Emotion will invariably lead to costly mistakes.

@OptionsHawk

Founder of http://OptionsHawk.com - Head of the Top Rated Live Trading Room - See Site for Subscription Service Plans.

Name:

Joe Kunkle

Website:

www.OptionsHawk.com

Email:

TradingHawk@gmail.com

How long have you been active investing or trading in the financial markets?

15 Years

What year did you become active on Twitter?

Services offered:

Live Market Coverage with a focus on large option trades and unusual trading patterns. Site provides full market coverage with fundamental, technical, and ownership analysis as well as proprietary trading tools and databases.

Which markets and instruments do you trade?

Equities and options

Why did you choose these markets?

These are the markets I know best.

What type of trader do you consider yourself?

Momentum Trader, Swing Trader, and Position Trader.

Do you have a target for your average annual returns?

Yes

What time frame do you prefer to trade in, and do you ever change time frames?

Every trade has its own time frame depending on the reason for initiating. Fundamental trades have longer time frames, while technical trades have price driven targets without a set time frame. Lastly, event-driven trades target a specific date.

What is the maximum drawdown you are willing to tolerate in pursuit of these returns?

15%

What technical indicators do you use to help quantify buy and sell signals?

Basic patterns such as flags and triangles. I utilize some RSI, MACD, OBV and moving averages, but simpler is better when it comes to technical analysis.

Are there any chart patterns you use for trading?

Flags, triangles, bases and trend lines.

What was your best trading year and what did you learn?

The best year was during the Financial Crisis. As an option trader, opportunities for profit increase with volatile markets, and options flow was signaling the banks were in trouble. There were plenty of days of 500%+ gains in put options on the banks.

What was your worst trading year and what did you learn?

The worst year was 2014 in terms of relative performance to the market. It was the first time I underperformed, as I got caught long into the October mini-crash. It was a great learning experience. It reminded me to keep a more balanced long/short portfolio and allowed me to significantly outperform the market and the majority of hedge funds in 2015.

How do you quantify your entry into a trade? What parameters do you use?

I have a 1-5 confidence rating per trade, and generally only take the 3-5 confidence rating trades unless I am speculating on an event-catalyst. Entry size is determined by that scale, and applied to the overall portfolio allocation rules.

How do you manage your exit from a trade? What parameters do you use?

In option trades, I tend to take at least 1/2 a position off after a 100% gain, allowing the rest of the trade to be a free trade. Otherwise, the majority of my trades target a specific catalyst/date, and exit once that event occurs.

What is your favorite trading quote?

"The secret to being successful from a trading perspective is to have an indefatigable and an undying and unquenchable thirst for information and knowledge." - Paul Tudor Jones

What are your favorite trading books?

"Trading Options at Expiration" by Jeff Augen, The Volatility Edge", "Day Trading Options", Kahn "Technical Analysis: Plain and Simple", Sinclair "Options Trading: Pricing and Volatility Strategies and Techniques", "Volatility Trading", Schwager's "Market Wizards".

Who are your favorite traders to follow on Twitter?

@BluegrassCap, @WolfMetric, @Optionstrader32, @Fzucchi, @Gtlackey

Who has influenced you the most on your trading journey?

I'm self-taught and have not been influenced by anyone.

What lessons have the markets taught you about yourself?

I've become so accustomed to winning that the wins no longer get me excited, but I hate losing more than ever.

What lessons have the markets taught you about other traders and investors?

The majority of traders let emotions control too many decisions, and also are not willing to adapt to changing markets and utilize new techniques.

What do you love about trading?

I love the learning aspect; being able to assess new information in real time, apply it, and make trades. I also love building new tools for in depth analysis of stocks.

What do you find to be the most difficult aspect of trading?

It takes a lot of work and dedication to be an active trader, and it takes a toll on your physical and mental health. I don't like being tied to desk so many hours throughout the week doing research, but find the more work you put in, the better the results.

What are the biggest mistakes that lead to a trader's unprofitability?

Thinking they know more about a stock than the market, and ignoring red flags in short interest trends and price-action. Not realizing a good company can be a bad stock, and a bad company can be a good stock. Listening to the media and sell-side reports, herd-like thinking.

What one piece of advice would you give to a new trader?

Be willing to work hard at your craft to develop a trading style and plan that best fits your personal goals and risk parameters. Utilize all the incredible tools available in this new financial technology age to assess companies/stocks from every angle, and be patient. Stocks tend to always come down to optimal entry levels.

@Peterghostine

Founder of 61point8 LLC. My evidence-driven methodology aims to identify and trade high-probability setups from both the long and short sides of the market.

Name:

Peter Ghostine

Website:

www.61point8.com

Email:

61point8@peterghostine.com

How long have you been active investing or trading in the financial markets?

Since 1998, but I got real serious in 2008. Most of what I know I've managed to learn during the last 8 years.

What year did you become active on Twitter?

2011

Services offered:

I offer an 'education and guidance' service dubbed 'TradeWinds'. It entails the following: ongoing technical analysis of the U.S. stock market. Real-time commentary via live meeting room from 8:30 a.m. to 4:00 p.m. daily, real-time trade alerts via Twitter, email, and my personal online trade book. My service is strictly educational and aims to help members develop a solid technical analysis foundation. It also teaches the *why* behind every trade I personally take, as well as the *how* (put/call options, debit/credit spreads). (Disclosure: I am not a certified investment advisor. My own trades are not recommendations.)

Which markets and instruments do you trade?

Index ETFs, index futures, momentum stocks.

Why did you choose these markets?

That's what I started with, and so I stayed the course. I've never been interested in currencies, commodities, etc.

What type of trader do you consider yourself?

Momentum Trader, Swing Trader, Trend Follower, and Day Trader.

Do you have a target for your average annual returns?

No

What time frame do you prefer to trade in, and do you ever change time frames?

Markets are fractal, and therefore trade setups are bound to present themselves on just about any time frame. For example, a head and shoulders pattern could setup on the weekly or daily time frame, thus requiring that it be swing-traded. Likewise, the same pattern on the 5-minute time frame would qualify as a day trading opportunity. The best swing trades are those found near prior major highs or lows, and on the heels of 80 or 90 percent up or down days. In general, I rarely ever keep a trade on for longer than 1 to 2 weeks, and so I'd much rather day trade, especially early in a newly established trend, and upon the failure of a crucial support or resistance level.

What is the maximum drawdown you are willing to tolerate in pursuit of these returns?

I wish the answer was as simple as a black and white. I've let some trades go completely bust in the past, just to prove a point, and I still managed a very healthy monthly return. At the end of the day, you want to protect your cash if you plan on being in the game for a long time.

What technical indicators do you use to help quantify buy and sell signals?

The more evidence in support of a trade, the better. In general, I keep things reasonably simple. At any given time, I may use some or all of the following: TREND (50-SMA, 15-EMA, Bollinger Bands), CYCLE (STOCHASTIC using non-default parameters), MOMENTUM (MACD using non-default parameters), SUPPORT/RESISTANCE (moving averages, prior highs/lows, high-volume area/point of control, gaps), PATTERNS (charts, candlesticks, Elliott Wave, and harmonic), and EXHAUSTION (Tom DeMark TD Sequential and Combo).

Are there any chart patterns you use for trading?

Classic chart patterns: head and shoulders, cup and handle, flags, triangles, etc.

Candlestick patterns: only a handful.

Harmonic patterns, Crab, Bat, Gartley, Shark, Cypher, 3 Drives, 5-0, etc.

Some Elliott Wave patterns that I've come to trust over time.

What was your best trading year and what did you learn?

2012 was a pivotal year that allowed me to get things back on track in 2013 and forward.

What was your worst trading year and what did you learn?

I've blown two accounts in the past, and that taught me that knowledge of technical analysis is nowhere near as important as objectivity, patience, and level-headedness. The more you learn, the more you realize how much more there is to learn. 2008-2010 were losing years for me. 2011 started off as a highly profitable year and ended up as the worst year ever.

How do you quantify your entry into a trade? What parameters do you use?

No two trades are ever the same, and I certainly don't try to 'split the atom' insofar my approach to entering a particular trade. To a great extent, I rely on instinct, and I don't necessarily always enter a trade 'mechanically' or at the 'ideal' entry point, like when one particular moving average crosses another, or upon a channel break, etc. Since my approach is evidence-based, I enter a trade when there's enough evidence in support of a given setup. Of course, the evidence is derived from those indicators I cited earlier. For example, is the current trend up or down? Is it exhausted? Is there a reversal pattern currently forming?

How do you manage your exit from a trade? What parameters do you use?

I try to exit a portion of the trade (partial exit, maybe 25% of it) upon reaching the first meaningful support or resistance level. I'm a strong advocate of keeping the trade on until a particular technical objective has been reached.

What is your favorite trading quote?

I honestly don't have a favorite one. But when I finally got a good grip on technical analysis years ago, it didn't take long for me to realize that *"When you have a hammer, everything looks like a nail."* I urge everyone to avoid this pitfall, as there's a lot more to trading than technical knowledge.

What are your favorite trading books?

I don't have a favorite 'trading' book. However, Edwards and Magee's "Technical Analysis of Stock Trends" remains my favorite technical analysis book. It has stood the test of time.

Who are your favorite traders to follow on Twitter?

I certainly favor those who turn a blind eye to adversity and strive to disseminate useful knowledge and information. To name a few, I like @HamzeiAnalytics, @ForexStopHunter, @Chirho23, @InterestRateArb, @1nvestor, and @Jfahmy. I must admit, though, that I've probably read less than 50 tweets in almost a year because I'm primarily focused on what I'm seeing and doing.

Who has influenced you the most on your trading journey?

Two traders that I've always looked up to for their technical analysis prowess are Tim Collins @RetroWallSt, and Bob Byrne @ByrneRWS. I've also incorporated much of what I've learned from Barry Burns @TopDogTrading, into my own framework.

What lessons have the markets taught you about yourself?

It exposed just about every flaw that I possess, including recklessness and ego. It taught me the value of patience, objectivity, and that what doesn't kill you *can* make you stronger.

What lessons have the markets taught you about other traders and investors?

That they all invariably learn the same hard lessons. Some pass, others fail. The best of them patiently wait for a trade opportunity like a deer hunter waits for a deer to come into his kill zone. The worst of them try to put down others to make themselves feel better.

What do you love about trading?

I'm not sure I love it to the extent that one could possibly love a job. However, I do get satisfaction from being able to decipher the price action and disseminate it in useful form that I and others could potentially benefit from.

What do you find to be the most difficult aspect of trading?

Having to learn and endure every hard lesson. I'm not sure there's a shortcut.

@RampCapitalLLC

Ramping up the market every day from 3:30-3:45pm.

Website:

www.330ramp.com

How long have you been active investing or trading in the financial markets?

8 years

What year did you become active on Twitter?

2009

Services offered:

I offer free Ramping services at 3:30-3:45 pm every day.

Which markets and instruments do you trade?

U.S. markets. Stocks and options.

Why did you choose these markets?

Because the USA is the greatest country in the world.

What type of trader do you consider yourself?

Other

Do you have a target for your average annual returns?

Yes

What time frame do you prefer to trade in, and do you ever change time frames?

3:30-3:45 pm ET. I change time frames when the American people need my help.

What is the maximum drawdown you are willing to tolerate in pursuit of these returns?

Drawdowns aren't in my vocabulary.

What technical indicators do you use to help quantify buy and sell signals?

The clock striking 3:30 pm.

Are there any chart patterns you use for trading?

No, that's voodoo.

What was your best trading year and what did you learn?

I don't remember my best and worst years. Everything has been great since 2009.

How do you quantify your entry into a trade? What parameters do you use?

I use a standard digital clock and proprietary algorithms.

How do you manage your exit from a trade? What parameters do you use?

The clock striking 3:45 pm.

What is your favorite trading quote?

"I'm so bullish it hurts."

What are your favorite trading books?

"The Quants" and "Dark Pools"

Who are your favorite traders to follow on Twitter?

Rudolph Havenstein, Wu Tang Finance, and Josh Brown

Who has influenced you the most on your trading journey?

Zerohedge and Nanex

What lessons have the markets taught you about yourself?

The market can make you look really smart and really dumb at the same time.

What lessons have the markets taught you about other traders and investors?

That a lot of people lie about their trades and no one will admit to a loss. Especially on Twitter.

What do you love about trading?

Getting rich and retiring early.

What do you find to be the most difficult aspect of trading?

Weeding through the bullshit.

What are the biggest mistakes that lead to a trader's unprofitability?

Listening to their brain instead of their gut.

What one piece of advice would you give to a new trader?

Follow me on Twitter.

@Rayner_Teo

Independent trader. Trend Follower. Helping traders succeed.

Name:

Rayner Teo

Website:

www.tradingwithrayner.com

Email:

tradingwithrayner@gmail.com

How long have you been active investing or trading in the financial markets?

8 years

What year did you become active on Twitter?

2015

Services offered:

Trend Following Mentorship Program

Which markets and instruments do you trade?

Forex and futures

Why did you choose these markets?

Because of the wide exposure to different sectors of the markets.

What type of trader do you consider yourself?

Trend Follower and Position Trader.

Do you have a target for your average annual returns?

Yes

What time frame do you prefer to trade in, and do you ever change time frames?

I enter primarily off the daily and 4-hour time frames, but when the market is trending strongly, I could even go down into 1 hour and 15-minutes to scale in my trades.

What is the maximum drawdown you are willing to tolerate in pursuit of these returns?

30%

What technical indicators do you use to help quantify buy and sell signals?

20, 50 and 200-day moving averages and Average true range (ATR). 20 and 50 to help identify dynamic support and resistance, 200 to help identify long term trend, and ATR to help set my stop loss based on volatility of the markets.

Are there any chart patterns you use for trading?

Continuation patterns like flags and pennants.

What was your best and worst trading year and what did you learn?

The first two years of trading was bad as I was trading without a plan.

The biggest mistake I made was hopping from one trading system to the next too quickly. I then learned the importance of being consistent in my actions in order to be a consistent trader. A trading plan would greatly help any trader.

How do you quantify your entry into a trade? What parameters do you use?

Price has to be above 200 MA for longs, and below 200 MA for shorts. If it's above 200 MA, I'll watch if price respects the 20 and 50 MA. If it does, I'll look to enter on the third retest when the candle closes higher from it.

How do you manage your exit from a trade? What parameters do you use?

If it's a swing trade, I'll just exit my position at the swing high/low in the market. If it's a trend following trade, I'll trail it using the moving average. Sometimes, I'll use the 20 MA, sometimes it's the 50 MA. This depends on the price action structure of the markets.

What is your favorite trading quote?

"The market is never too high to long, or too low to short."

What are your favorite trading books?

Market Wizards, Reminiscences of a Stock Operator, Trend Following, The Art and, Science of Technical Analysis, Trading in the Zone.

Who are your favorite traders to follow on Twitter?

Steve Burns, Rolf from Tradeciety, Assad Tannousm, Tom Dantem, and Lance Beggs.

Who has influenced you the most on your trading journey?

The Turtle Traders, Jesse Livermore, and Ed Seykota.

What lessons have the markets taught you about yourself?

The markets have taught me that I'm actually a patient trader who has no problems sitting on his hands, so trading the higher time frames suits my personality better. On a side note, I tend to overthink a lot so I faced the issue of analysis paralysis in my early years of trading. Now, I keep things as simple as possible.

What lessons have the markets taught you about other traders and investors?

There's more than one way to skin a cat. There are traders who use the order flow, traders who do well using technical analysis, and traders who do well with fundamental analysis only. Losing traders don't have a plan. They enter a trade and pray for the best. Winning traders always have a plan. It's all about finding a trading approach that suits you. There's no right or wrong method, but what suits you best.

What do you love about trading?

The fact that you're in an industry where 95% of traders lose. It gives me a whole new perspective on life, and towards risk.

What do you find to be the most difficult aspect of trading?

Finding an edge and having the conviction to stay with your strategy when the going gets tough. Most traders would abandon their strategy altogether and find something else. Pro traders would reduce risk and reflect on how they could perform better.

What are the biggest mistakes that lead to a trader's unprofitability?

Hopping from one system to the next, trading without a plan, undercapitalization, and having the wrong expectations.

What one piece of advice would you give to a new trader?

Focus on doing the right thing and the money will take care of itself. Start really small because you're going to be a horrible trader at the start. Keep your "tuition fees" low by trading small.

@Reddogt3

Chief Strategist T3Live/T3TradingGroup, frequent CNBC/Bloomberg/Fox Biz guest, IronMan, devoted Husband & Father.

Name:

Scott Redler

Website:

www.T3live.com

Email:

Scott@t3live.com

How long have you been active investing or trading in the financial markets?

Almost 20 years

What year did you become active on Twitter?

2013

Services offered:

I write a note each morning. It's my active plan to the market each day with sectors and names.

Which markets and instruments do you trade?

Mostly equities.

Why did you choose these markets?

They are liquid and move fast.

What type of trader do you consider yourself?

Momentum Trader, Swing Trader, Trend Follower, Day Trader, and Position Trader.

Do you have a target for your average annual returns?

No

What time frame do you prefer to trade in, and do you ever change time frames?

I approach the market on multiple time frames. But I actively trade for alpha and cash flow on an intermediate basis.

What is the maximum drawdown you are willing to tolerate in pursuit of these returns?

Depends on the market, but I look for paper cuts and not gushers.

What technical indicators do you use to help quantify buy and sell signals?

I use moving averages, chart patterns, and pivots.

Are there any chart patterns you use for trading?

Yes, all of them.

What was your best and worst trading year and what did you learn?

Last year, 2015, was very tough. You had to buy when they felt bad and sell when they looked good. Bad for momentum traders.

How do you quantify your entry into a trade? What parameters do you use?

It all depends on the day and the market.

How do you manage your exit from a trade? What parameters do you use?

I try and look for resistance 1-2-3 and/or when the trade changes.

What is your favorite trading quote?

"Trade what you see, not what you want to see."

What are your favorite trading books?

"The Modern Trader", "How to Make Money in Stocks", and "Trading in the Zone."

Who are your favorite traders to follow on Twitter?

Too many to name.

Who has influenced you the most on your trading journey?

Dan Zanger

What lessons have the markets taught you about yourself?

That you always need to evolve and trust your inner trading voice. You can't be perfect.

What lessons have the markets taught you about other traders and investors?

I don't like traders who aren't accountable for their actions, or those that are irresponsible and try and make headlines.

What do you love about trading?

The sky is the limit. It's ultimately up to our own ability and effort.

What do you find to be the most difficult aspect of trading?

Doing what your inner voice says. Not acting on what you think is going to happen.

What are the biggest mistakes that lead to a trader's unprofitability?

Listening to noise and not trusting their instincts. Trading for an amount of money versus what the market is giving.

What one piece of advice would you give to a new trader?

It's a blue collar job that is not a get rich quick scheme. It takes time and a process.

@Sharptraders

Trade What's Happening...Not What You Think Is Gonna Happen.

Name:

Doug Gregory

Website:

http://sharptraders.com

Email:

doug@sharptraders.com

How long have you been active investing or trading in the financial markets?

30+ years

What year did you become active on Twitter?

2009

Services offered:

Free stock lists, charts, and trading tools.

Which markets and instruments do you trade?

U.S. stocks and ETFs.

Why did you choose these markets?

Just grew up with them.

What type of trader do you consider yourself?

Momentum Trader and Day Trader.

Do you have a target for your average annual returns?

No

What time frame do you prefer to trade in, and do you ever change time frames?

Minutes up to an hour.

What is the maximum drawdown you are willing to tolerate in pursuit of these returns?

Not much.

What technical indicators do you use to help quantify buy and sell signals?

Primarily SLO STO (5,3), TRIX (5,2), and ADX (7).

Are there any chart patterns you use for trading?

Flags and J-Hooks.

What was your best trading year and what did you learn?

Best year was +101% in 1999. Not much that I use now.

What was your worst year and what did you learn?

Worst year was +1% in 2002. Don't try to outsmart the markets.

How do you quantify your entry into a trade? What parameters do you use?

Wait for pullbacks and subsequent moves on volume.

How do you manage your exit from a trade? What parameters do you use?

When it stops going up I sell.

What is your favorite trading quote?

"Trade what's happening, not what you think is gonna happen."

What are your favorite trading books?

"Encyclopedia of Chart patterns" by Bulkowski, "How to Make Money in Stocks" by O'Neil, and "Guide to The Markets", by Investor's Business Daily.

Who are your favorite traders to follow on Twitter?

Too many...I don't want to leave anyone out.

Who has influenced you the most on your trading journey?

My dad.

What lessons have the markets taught you about yourself?

Patience and focus.

What lessons have the markets taught you about other traders and investors?

Don't believe everything you read.

What do you love about trading?

Analysis, and of course, making money.

What do you find to be the most difficult aspect of trading?

Waiting for the trade to come to you.

What are the biggest mistakes that lead to a trader's unprofitability?

Believing a stock just has to come back, and the desire to be right

What one piece of advice would you give to a new trader?

Do not try to mimic other traders. Be aware of what good traders are doing, but develop your own style.

@SJosephBurns

Trend and swing Trader, risk manager, and best-selling trading author. Daily blogger at NewTraderU. Helping new traders survive and become profitable.

Name:

Steve Burns

Services offered:

I blog daily at NewTraderU.com, write affordable trading books, and have create e-courses for new traders.

Website:

www.NewTraderU.com

Email:

Stephen@newtraderu.com

How long have you been active investing or trading in the financial markets?

I have been active in the market for 25 years.

What year did you become active on Twitter?

2010

Which markets and instruments do you trade?

I trade the stock market with leveraged ETFs, index ETFs, index mutual funds, growth stocks, and stock options.

Why did you choose these markets?

I like the simplicity of the stock market and its natural bullish bias over the long term. Stocks go through cycles of accumulation and distribution, and I think it's simpler to trade than commodities or forex markets.

What type of trader do you consider yourself?

Swing Trader

Do you have a target for your average annual returns?

Yes

What time frame do you prefer to trade in, and do you ever change time frames?

I prefer to trade off the daily chart but I will look at the intraday range to time entries and exits. I trade price swings inside the longer term trend. I will hold trades for days and weeks in the right trend. I will also day trade and stop holding over night when volatility is high.

What is the maximum drawdown you are willing to tolerate in pursuit of these returns?

My goal is a 5% maximum drawdown in a year. I am usually able to achieve that.

What technical indicators do you use to help quantify buy and sell signals?

I trade using price support and resistance levels, moving averages, MACD, RSI, and ATR. I will buy and sell based on a horizontal trend line that establishes support or resistance. Moving averages filter the trend in different time frames for me. The MACD crossovers can show me turning points in a trend. The RSI is my overbought and oversold indicator. The ATR helps with position sizing and reversion to the mean trades on extensions from key moving averages.

Are there any chart patterns you use for trading?

Flags, triangles, and pennants do a great job visually representing the ranges I am watching. I like rectangles that show support and resistance and breakouts of ranges.

What was your best trading year and what did you learn?

My best year was 2012. I had a +52% return in the first quarter alone thanks to trading the Apple and Priceline breakouts to all-time highs with weekly call options.

What was your worst trading year and what did you learn?

2000-2002 were the years. They taught me that markets can go down as well as up. I ended up with a +50% drawdown from my equity peak by 2003. Perma-bull is not a strategy because markets change. It took me a few years to get back to where I was in March of 2000.

How do you quantify your entry into a trade? What parameters do you use?

I use multiple parameters to enter trades. I want to see signals align. Some filters for buying are: price above the 10-day EMA and 200 day SMA, RSI above 30, MACD bullish crossover, and higher highs and higher lows. I will also buy when an index is extended from the 10 day EMA by 1.5 to 2 ATR.

How do you manage your exit from a trade? What parameters do you use?

I will exit a winning trade when it hits my profit target. This is usually around a key level of resistance. Or I will exit a winning trade when it reverses and closes near a key, short term moving average. I will exit a losing trade when my stop loss is hit at the level that shows I was wrong about the entry.

What is your favorite trading quote?

"It's not whether you're right or wrong that's important, but how much money you make when you're right and how much you lose when you're wrong." -George Soros

What are your favorite trading books?

"Trading for a Living" by Alexander Elder, "Trend Following" by Michael Covel, "Trade Like a Casino" by Richard Weissman, and Jack Schwager's "Market Wizards".

Who are your favorite traders to follow on Twitter?

I believe @Canuck2usa is the best trader I have seen through live calls on social media. I also really enjoy the content produced by @Tradeciety, he is like a Wikipedia for traders.

The most entertaining guy I follow is @NorthmanTrader. A lot of what I do on Twitter I learned from watching him.

Who has influenced you the most on your trading journey?

My biggest trading influences have been Alexander Elder, Michael Covel, Van Tharp, Jack Schwager's books, Paul Tudor Jones, Richard Weissman, and Dean Karrys. Meeting Paul Tudor Jones is on my bucket list.

What lessons have the markets taught you about yourself?

I was too aggressive with position sizing for years. I was overconfident in my ability to be right about a signal, and traded too big out of greed. I have learned that each trade is just one of the next 100, and I have to keep a consistent position size to avoid big drawdowns when I am wrong.

What lessons have the markets taught you about other traders and investors?

Many traders try to predict the future and then try to prove they're right. Their lack of flexibility can quickly get them on the wrong side of a trend. Investors struggle to separate the company that they like from the company's stock that may not be a good investment.

What do you love about trading?

I love the earning potential of trading, and I enjoy the game of trying to outwit other traders in one of the toughest games there is.

What do you find to be the most difficult aspect of trading?

Trading is tough because the profits are irregular and you can work hard for a long time only to lose money in the end. I hate to lose money, and that helps me take stop losses without hesitation. The whole point is to make money. I can always get back in.

What are the biggest mistakes that lead to a trader's unprofitability?

Position sizing and risk management. Traders tend to trade too big and risk too much, so their first losing streak is usually their last. They also tend to trade without a trading plan, so most of their results are just luck or market environment. The trading profits that come from luck usually go back to the traders with skill.

What one piece of advice would you give to a new trader?

Don't start trading until you have educated yourself about trading. Have a trading plan, a trading system, and a process with an edge before you place your first trade.

@Sssvenky

Name:

Venky Srinivasan

Website:

http://www.venkysrinivasan.com

Email:

venky@venkysrinivasan.com

How long have you been active investing or trading in the financial markets?

11 years

What year did you become active on Twitter?

2009

Services offered:

No, not yet. All content provided on StockTwits and Twitter have been free. However, I will be starting a premium service with recap and some trading ideas.

Which markets and instruments do you trade?

Stocks, bonds, Forex, futures, and options.

Why did you choose these markets?

They're the most liquid.

What type of trader do you consider yourself?

Swing Trader

Do you have a target for your average annual returns?

Yes

What time frame do you prefer to trade in, and do you ever change time frames?

Usually a 1-3 week time frame for longer swings. 1-3 days for quick swings. With the current market environment, I'm day trading mainly futures as they are easier to handle.

What is the maximum drawdown you are willing to tolerate in pursuit of these returns?

2-3%

What technical indicators do you use to help quantify buy and sell signals?

RSI, MACD, Slow STO and price with volume confirmation. Nothing more is needed. Believer of price action only.

Are there any chart patterns you use for trading?

No real chart patterns that I like, but I do like a descending channel or a symmetrical wedge. Also a few harmonic patterns for confirmation.

What was your best and worst trading year and what did you learn?

2008 was the worst and 2013 was the best. I learned to be patient and disciplined, follow price and volume for confirmation, turn off radio and TV especially, CNBC. You don't need anything more than this.

How do you quantify your entry into a trade? What parameters do you use?

Here's a link for what I look for (Risk Management & Trade Plan): http://venkysrinivasan.com/successfultrade-plan/

How do you manage your exit from a trade? What parameters do you use?

Here's a link for what I look for (Risk Management & Trade Plan): http://venkysrinivasan.com/successfultrade-plan/

What is your favorite trading quote?

"Risk comes from not knowing what you are doing." - Warren Buffet

What are your favorite trading books?

My two favorite books are "Using Technical Analysis to Design Winning Trades" by Greg Harmon and "Technical Analysis Using Multiple Time Frames" by Brian Shannon.

Here's a list of many trading books that I've reviewed - great list by Brian Lund. http://bclund.com/2012/03/13/20-books-every-trader-should-know/

Who are your favorite traders to follow on Twitter?

http://venkysrinivasan.com/top-stocktwits-traders/

Who has influenced you the most on your trading journey?

Greg Harmon, Howard Lindzon, and Brian Shannon.

What lessons have the markets taught you about yourself?

Have a sound risk management plan and trading plan. Do your homework every evening/night before the next trading day (support/resistance/pivots/Fibs). Follow price action and cut noise. Be disciplined and be patient. You don't have to trade every day to make money. Sitting on your hands is an art, and practice that more often.

What lessons have the markets taught you about other traders and investors?

Follow price action and cut noise. Be disciplined and be patient. Be humble and a silent listener, ask questions in a very polite way.

What do you love about trading?

If one is disciplined and has a plan for managing risk, it gives you a great perspective for how to manage money and risk in day to day life. You don't have to be a management guru or IT guru to know that.

What do you find to be the most difficult aspect of trading?

Patience.

What are the biggest mistakes that lead to a trader's unprofitability?

Blindly following others into a trade without their sound risk management plan. Listening to radio, CNBC etc., making predictions beyond their control.

What one piece of advice would you give to a new trader?

Be patient, disciplined, follow price action and turn off the noise. Don't chase and don't be biased when trading. Being open minded goes a long way in a long term trading career.

@StockCats

Stock Trader, Speculator, Technical Anarchist, Financial Media Critic. I work hard so my cats can have a better life.

Website:

http://www.stockcats.com

How long have you been active investing or trading in the financial markets?

Roughly 4 of 9-lives.

What year did you become active on Twitter?

2009

Services offered:

None, I'm just here to have fun.

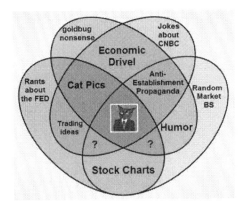

Which markets and instruments do you trade?

Stocks and ETF's at the moment, and quite possibly ES Futures in the near future.

Why did you choose these markets?

Stocks are easy to understand and I like simplicity.

What type of trader do you consider yourself?

Swing Trader and Day Trader.

Do you have a target for your average annual returns?

No

What time frame do you prefer to trade in, and do you ever change time frames?

A few minutes to a few days depending on the setup. I use a combination of day trading and swing trading, depending on what I see on the charts and the current environment.

What is the maximum drawdown you are willing to tolerate in pursuit of these returns?

Stops are based on levels I see on the charts. For a swing trade I like setups that offer roughly a 4-6% stop.

What technical indicators do you use to help quantify buy and sell signals?

RSI, MACD, moving averages, trend lines, and DMI Oscillator.

Are there any chart patterns you use for trading?

Just about all of them, including similar patterns that seem to repeat on a particular stock.

What were your best and worst trading years and what did you learn?

The first couple years I started "investing" were probably the worst. I held stocks through big ups and downs and let profits turn into losses. I held on until I eventually got tired of holding and sold. Some with profits and some with losses. I realized that investing and trading were two different things and buying and holding wasn't really what I wanted to do. With limited capital, the "opportunity cost" of just holding a stock was holding me back.

How do you quantify your entry into a trade? What parameters do you use?

For swings, I look for setups on the daily time frame, then typically use the 15-minute or 60-minute chart for entries based on the price action in relation to the 20 and 50 period EMAs and trend line breaks. One of the first things I look for is a reasonable level to set a top based on a prior price level.

How do you manage your exit from a trade? What parameters do you use?

It's on a case by case basis but I like to have an initial target in mind and then either take 1/2 off the table or trail up a stop. I never trade in the first 5-15 minutes of the day and honestly prefer to be patient and gauge market behavior in the morning session and look for opportunities later in the day.

What is your favorite trading quote?

"Don't fight the tape."

What are your favorite trading books?

I read so many books years ago that I barely remember any of them, but "How to Make Money in Stocks" by William O'Neil is the one I always recommend.

Who are your favorite traders to follow on Twitter?

That's an impossible question for me because I do my own thing as far as scans, setups and stock ideas. I'm mostly on Twitter to have fun.

Who has influenced you the most on your trading journey?

My Father. The first thing he told me about the stock market is "never listen to anyone".

What lessons have the markets taught you about yourself?

So many times when I "thought" the market was going to do something it did something different. I learned that the market seldom does what I want it to do so I have to trade based on what I see happening - not on what I think will happen.

What lessons have the markets taught you about other traders and investors?

No one knows nuthin' ™ Just kidding, everyone has to develop their own style and trade based on their own time frame. To me "time frame" is one of the most important, yet least discussed aspects of this business. Also, people tend to have an emotional relationship with a stock they own, which I understand, but have learned to avoid this.

What do you love about trading?

I love looking through charts. I look through charts day and night, every day and every night, and never tire of it. I really enjoy the geometry of price patterns and after all these years I just see things on the charts.

What do you find to be the most difficult aspect of trading?

The overnight gaps and uncertainty surrounding earnings releases. In recent years it seems like more and more of a crap-shoot on where a stock I hold overnight may open. Holding over earnings is most definitely a crap-shoot and I avoid that completely.

What are the biggest mistakes that lead to a trader's unprofitability?

Obviously, not setting a stop and letting a trade get away from them. Stops are one of the only ways we have to mitigate risk and many people don't seem to realize that if a stop gets hit you can always buy the stock back, and many times at a better price.

What one piece of advice would you give to a new trader?

Pay the utmost attention to the directional move off today's open. The "smoke screen" they use to obfuscate everyone, is comparing where a stock or market's price is in relation to yesterday's close instead of today's open.

@SunriseTrader

Trader trading the trend. Trade in a state of grace. Family, friends, laughter, health, and time to play are important to me. Living life in alignment with 'what is'.

How long have you been active investing or trading in the financial markets?

Too many years to mention the exact year.

What year did you become active on Twitter?

2009

Which markets and instruments do you trade?

Equities/common stock, all exchanges, NO pink sheets/over the counter stocks.

Why did you choose these markets?

Liquidity

What type of trader do you consider yourself?

Swing Trader

Do you have a target for your average annual returns?

Yes

What time frame do you prefer to trade in, and do you ever change time frames?

For swing trading, I prefer using the daily chart and then 60-65 minute charts. At times, weekly/monthly. For day trading, 30-15-5 minute and occasionally 60-65 minute charts.

What is the maximum drawdown you are willing to tolerate in pursuit of these returns?

Stops are set based on a variety of factors and not one drawdown amount for all trades.

What technical indicators do you use to help quantify buy and sell signals?

Price, price, and price first and foremost. I use the MACD and RSI indicators on daily/weekly/monthly charts. I sometimes use Stochastic indicator. I prefer to keep oscillators to a minimum as not to be paralyzed by over analysis. Keeping my charts simple.

Are there any chart patterns you use for trading?

Positive and negative divergences on the oscillators accompanied by the appropriate candle signal.

What was your best and worst trading year and what did you learn?

The beginning years I had a learning curve of errors by thinking and not using my eyes. Once I understood how to read the charts and their story, my trading went to the next level and I became a profitable trader with few errors. I am blessed with patience and steel nerves naturally which helped with the emotional side of trading. My best trading years are bull market trends that are clear to read.

How do you quantify your entry into a trade? What parameters do you use?

I use a formula based on my personal style and the charts. The risk/reward potential must be in my favor. I often buy at support with the appropriate oscillator and candle signal at levels that some don't want to touch the stock at, and sell part of my position to those chasing once the stock gets rocking. I like to leave one last piece on to let it 'seek its own level' by protecting the profits, raising the stop as the trade moves along. Patience for my style of trading is key. I use the *safety first* method.

How do you manage your exit from a trade? What parameters do you use?

I manage my exit using a ladder system. I like a quick payday on the first day of an up move in a trade. I will use resistance levels and a shorter time frame chart to determine the payday. When I put on a trade, I use a personal money management formula to decide how many shares are appropriate for a swing trade, and I will add additional knowing I am taking a quick payday and will be down to swing size. My ladder method is not equal parts on each rung of the ladder.

What is your favorite trading quote?

As a trader my job is to manage risk, consistently take profits out of the market while preserving emotional and financial capital. -SunriseTrader

What are your favorite trading books?

"The StockTwits Edge" and "Trading in the Zone".

Who are your favorite traders to follow on Twitter?

My total stream for various reasons. Some great traders, some contrarian traders, some just nice folks. I know there are many more I should follow.

Who has influenced you the most on your trading journey?

Many

What lessons have the markets taught you about yourself?

Discipline and patience are key and I am naturally blessed with both. Trading has honed the skill and reinforced the need for both.

What lessons have the markets taught you about other traders and investors?

That trading is not one size fits all. Trading has many styles and all can be profitable. One must find their own edge and style. Keep it simple. Wash, rinse, repeat.

What do you love about trading?

The hunt using my own intellect and skills, the responsibility of my own success, and the freedom.

What do you find to be the most difficult aspect of trading?

The noise, be it from news, economic reports, or others.

What are the biggest mistakes that lead to a trader's unprofitability?

Not taking a loss. Thinking too much about the money and not the skill of the trade. Fear. Always having to be right. Ego. No trading plan. Poor or non-existent money management skills.

What one piece of advice would you give to a new trader?

Slow down, trading is a marathon and not a sprint.

@Tradeciety

Trading Blog & Website- www.tradeciety.com | Partner-site of www.edgewonk.com. Daily trading tips | No investment advice.

Website:

www.tradeciety.com

Email:

rolf@tradeciety.com

How long have you been active investing or trading in the financial markets?

+-7 years

What year did you become active on Twitter?

2014

Services offered:

Tradeciety is a non-commercial trading blog covering all aspects of day and swing trading. Edgewonk is a trading journal and a trader development tool.

Which markets and instruments do you trade?

90% Forex and 10% DAX.

Why did you choose these markets?

Forex for the fundamental and macro aspect. Together with technical analysis, it makes for an ideal trading environment.

What type of trader do you consider yourself?

Swing Trader

Do you have a target for your average annual returns?

No

What time frame do you prefer to trade in, and do you ever change time frames?

Daily and 4-hour for analysis. Mostly 4-hour for entry timing and rarely 1-hour to analyze market micro structures.

What is the maximum drawdown you are willing to tolerate in pursuit of these returns?

2R daily. 7% on a month to month basis.

What technical indicators do you use to help quantify buy and sell signals?

RSI and Bollinger Bands exclusively. Bollinger Bands to identify over-extended trends and price extremes. RSI to mark fading momentum around extreme tops and bottoms.

Are there any chart patterns you use for trading?

I am mainly a reversal trader, looking for unsustainable trends so I use head and shoulders patterns. I analyze trend line breaks and the shifting powers of buying and selling pressure around market extremes.

What was your best and worst trading year and what did you learn?

2014 was one of my best trading years. It's the year when I completely abandoned any return goals. I started approaching the markets from a perspective where I became extremely selective, only looking to get 3/4 trades per month. Trading without having to trade is the most liberating thing you can do for yourself, and it helps with the mental aspect. When I started building other income streams besides trading, it took away a lot of pressure which also impacted my performance a lot. I attribute a lot of the good returns to avoiding mental pressure and not having to trade.

How do you quantify your entry into a trade? What parameters do you use?

It starts with fundamental analysis, where I determine the general direction and also select the markets I trade. I then drill down from a technical perspective. I look for over-extended trends and unsustainable moves. I use Fibonacci extensions to locate likely turning points, and I look for support and demand imbalances at potential turning points. I wait for volatility spikes at my adjusted Bollinger Bands, preferably with momentum divergences. This happens on the Daily and 4-hour. Once I have identified key turn areas, I wait for price to get there and then look for transitions. Specifically, for a breakdown of market structures. I prefer double tops with false breakouts, or "messy" head and shoulders patterns to signal a momentum change.

How do you manage your exit from a trade? What parameters do you use?

I aim at a 2R profit but I am prepared to let it run. I mainly use supply and demand zones to pinpoint exits, but I use a moving average to analyze momentum shifts. I prefer to cut my trade very quickly when I see it's going against me. As I mentioned above, I never feel an urge to trade, and I'm comfortable with not trading for weeks when I don't see anything interesting. I really only need 3 trades per month.

What is your favorite trading quote?

"Most traders take a good system and destroy it by trying to make it into a perfect system." – Robert Prechter

"Instead of hoping he must fear; instead of fearing he must hope. He must fear that his loss must develop into a much bigger loss, and hope that his profit may become a big profit." -Jesse Livermore

What are your favorite trading books?

"Pit Bull: Lessons from Wall Street's Champion Day Trader", "Against the Gods: The Remarkable Story of Risk", "Gambling Wizards: Conversations with the World's Greatest Gamblers."

Who are your favorite traders to follow on Twitter?

Assad Tannous, Trader Dante, Steve Burns, and Dr. Steenbarger.

Who has influenced you the most on your trading journey?

I think I have re-read Marty Schwartz's book a dozen times. I am impressed with his work ethic and how obsessed he is about his preparation and analysis. This has influenced me significantly.

What lessons have the markets taught you about yourself?

I was (and still am) a very impatient person and I like to get things done. This cost me a lot of money in the beginning. I had an urge to be in a trade at all times. I noticed that I'm the same way outside of trading, and I'm now much more self-aware. It was a very painful journey because trading shows you who you are on a daily basis. But it also offers great learning experiences and promotes the need for self-improvement.

What lessons have the markets taught you about other traders and investors?

I don't want this to sound harsh, but the main thing I see daily is that most traders deserve to lose, because they just don't approach trading serious enough. I have said that I don't need to trade as often, and most people translate that into meaning that I don't put in the hours. I do most of my trading work away from the charts and it's normal for me to work 12 or 14 hour days. Most people think that 2 hours every day is enough, but it isn't. You hear people every day saying that the markets are so tough, but they really aren't. People just don't have what it takes and they are trading for the wrong reasons.

What do you love about trading?

I love the combination of macros and technicals. I can get lost in reading reports, sifting through speeches, and data analysis and then come up with macro theories and fundamental scenarios. When I can combine a fundamental trade idea with a technical setup, that's where I find enjoyment and that's what defines trading for me. I am also a *huge* numbers freak and I love to crunch my performance data and analyze every little aspect of my trading. I've always had a passion for math, and I can spend hours over spreadsheets analyzing data. Trading is the perfect mix for me between a mental game and the statistical aspect.

What do you find to be the most difficult aspect of trading?

The need to perform at a high level every day. Trading is a performance game, and if you're not aware of your current state, you can end up losing big time. I still struggle with this from time to time; I lose an unnecessary amount of money on a single trade, but I am mostly aware of why it happens. Making the constant effort to overcome those mental hurdles is what I'm working on most these days. But the more I dig into it, the more I realize that it's nothing you can eliminate completely.

What are the biggest mistakes that lead to a trader's unprofitability?

A lack of discipline. Not putting in the work necessary. Trading for the wrong reasons. Always wanting to trade. Changing their approach all the time.

What one piece of advice would you give to a new trader?

Audit yourself if you really want to do this. There are hundreds of ways to make money more easily. if you don't have a passion for trading, and I don't mean the gambling aspect, then don't even think of starting. If you are willing to work 30 or 40 hours a week besides your regular 9-5, then you might have a chance.

@Traderstewie

10 Day FREE Trial http://ArtOfTrading.net Premium Service! Visit my blog:
http://theimpatienttrader.blogspot.com.

Website:

www.Artoftrading.net

Email:

Traderstewie@gmail.com

How long have you been active investing or trading in the financial markets?

Active since 1997

What year did you become active on Twitter?

2009

Which markets and instruments do you trade?

Equities and ETFs.

Why did you choose these markets?

They vibe with my style. Especially ETFs which carry less risk (more predictability than individual stocks).

What type of trader do you consider yourself?

Momentum Trader and Day Trader.

Do you have a target for your average annual returns?

No

What time frame do you prefer to trade in, and do you ever change time frames?

I trade mostly 5-minutes charts in volatile markets but prefer daily charts.

What is the maximum drawdown you are willing to tolerate in pursuit of these returns?

1% of capital as a maximum acceptable daily loss.

What technical indicators do you use to help quantify buy and sell signals?

I like to use mostly just price action but I've found MACD, RSI to be helpful.

Are there any chart patterns you use for trading?

Falling wedges, rising wedges, double bottoms/tops. All for intraday charts.

What was your best and worst trading year and what did you learn?

Most important lesson by far was figuring out what was my maximum daily loss threshold. Stop trading once that threshold has been crossed. 'If it's Not Your Day, Walk Away'

How do you quantify your entry into a trade? What parameters do you use?

I like to buy steep pullbacks in ETFs like SPY and DIA as they wedge on intraday charts. Or short steep run-ups that wedge in these ETFs.

How do you manage your exit from a trade? What parameters do you use?

I tend to book gains very quickly. Often times exiting too soon, but there's no such thing as a perfect exit in trading. Take what the market is willing to give you and move on.

What is your favorite trading quote?

"Great traders understand the difference between looking for a trade and seeing the trade. Remain patient, they always come. When they do it's obvious." -Assad Tannous

What are your favorite trading books?

"Master Swing Trader" by Alan Farley, "Street Smarts" by Linda Raschke, and "Market Wizards" is also good.

Who are your favorite traders to follow on Twitter?

Too many to list.

Who has influenced you the most on your trading journey?

Traders like Steve Burns, I hold in high regard.

What lessons have the markets taught you about yourself?

Have to be incredibly persistent and thick skinned to keep going at it, and surviving the ever changing learning curve.

What lessons have the markets taught you about other traders and investors?

Human nature always does the thing when it's most emotional. The trader's emotions are his own worst enemy.

What do you love about trading?

It's never boring and I'm my own boss. It comes at a price though, since it's one of the hardest jobs you'll ever do. It'll test you in every way imaginable.

What do you find to be the most difficult aspect of trading?

It can be incredibly stressful. Controlling emotions during stressful periods can be challenging.

What are the biggest mistakes that lead to a trader's unprofitability?

The biggest mistake most traders make is they don't have proper risk control parameters, so as a result, they can suffer big losses in a short period. That's a painful lesson to learn the hard way. Ask yourself, if this trade busts, how much am I willing to lose?

What one piece of advice would you give to a new trader?

Watch and follow the good traders on Twitter. The honest traders too. Learn from their journeys and stories.

@WallStJesus

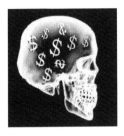

I am the way, the truth, and the life. No one can come to the Father except through me | Son of the Market Gods | Visit site for premium memberships & updates.

Website:

www.wallstjesus.com

How long have you been active investing or trading in the financial markets?

20+ years

What year did you become active on Twitter?

2011

Services offered:

Subscription to private twitter feed and chat.

Which markets and instruments do you trade?

Stocks and options.

Why did you choose these markets?

To try and make some $$.

What type of trader do you consider yourself?

Day Trader

Do you have a target for your average annual returns?

No

What time frame do you prefer to trade in, and do you ever change time frames?

Intraday

What is the maximum drawdown you are willing to tolerate in pursuit of these returns?

1-2%

What technical indicators do you use to help quantify buy and sell signals?

Options flow.

Are there any chart patterns you use for trading?

Not really.

What was your best trading year and what did you learn?

Don't know off hand but I learn every day.

How do you quantify your entry into a trade? What parameters do you use?

Don't chase.

How do you manage your exit from a trade? What parameters do you use?

Always lock up a profit, never fall in love, stick to your stops/plan.

What is your favorite trading quote?

You have to learn how to lose in order to learn how to win.

What are your favorite trading books?

Don't have a favorite.

Who are your favorite traders to follow on Twitter?

Too many to list.

Who has influenced you the most on your trading journey?

The market itself.

What lessons have the markets taught you about yourself?

That with a designed game plan/approach, I really can be disciplined.

What lessons have the markets taught you about other traders and investors?

They have no plan.

What do you love about trading?

The action.

What do you find to be the most difficult aspect of trading?

Wanting to trade and getting roped into all that action.

What are the biggest mistakes that lead to a trader's unprofitability?

No plan and no structure. Concentrating on trying to make money rather than on risk

What one piece of advice would you give to a new trader?

Don't even start without a plan that defines your risk.

@WeeklyOptTrader

Once U follow me u r stuck with me. For trading ideas register at http://awesometrading.net.

Website:

http://www.awesometrading.net

Services offered:

Stock and Options real time trades

Email:

awesometrading@yahoo.com

How long have you been active investing or trading in the financial markets?

8 years

What year did you become active on Twitter?

2013

Which markets and instruments do you trade?

US market: $AAPL, $AMZN, $BIDU, $BABA, $FB, $GOOGL, $HLF, $LNKD, $MNST, $NFLX, $PCLN, $TSLA, $TWTR, and $VRX.

Why did you choose these markets?

I follow a few stocks and master them. The reasons for choosing these stocks is that they move significantly intraday, providing good opportunity for option day trading.

What type of trader do you consider yourself?

Momentum Trader, Swing Trader, Trend Follower, and Day Trader.

Do you have a target for your average annual returns?

Yes

What time frame do you prefer to trade in, and do you ever change time frames?

Most of the trades last for 1-3 days. Few swing options trades last for a month.

What is the maximum drawdown you are willing to tolerate in pursuit of these returns?

2% per trade

What technical indicators do you use to help quantify buy and sell signals?

Chart patterns. Support and resistance from daily closing prices and from trend lines.

Are there any chart patterns you use for trading?

Symmetrical triangle, head and shoulder, inverted head and shoulder, pennant formation, ascending triangles, and descending triangles.

What was your best and worst trading year and what did you learn?

Worst year: First year of blowing up account.

Best year: 300% return (2015).

How do you quantify your entry into a trade? What parameters do you use?

Candle sentiment, volume, breakout levels, and chart patterns.

How do you manage your exit from a trade? What parameters do you use?

Options trading is best done by position sizing. Options can have huge % moves in both directions, so putting % stop loss usually doesn't work.

What is your favorite trading quote?

"It's when you're winning that you are most susceptible to making a mistake, overtrading, putting on too large a position." Mark Douglas

What are your favorite trading books?

"Trading in the Zone" by Mark Douglas

Who are your favorite traders to follow on Twitter?

@SJosephBurns, @Traderstewie, and @RedDogT3.

Who has influenced you the most on your trading journey?

Learned through real trades. Mark Douglas's "trading in the zone" did help a lot.

What lessons have the markets taught you about yourself?

Discipline, patience, and managing risk.

What lessons have the markets taught you about other traders and investors?

Most of the traders blow up their account due to poor risk management and being undisciplined.

What do you love about trading?

Chart analysis.

What do you find to be the most difficult aspect of trading?

Restraining yourself from entering into trades too soon.

What are the biggest mistakes that lead to a trader's unprofitability?

Trading too big a size on a single trade. Risk management is absolutely critical.

What one piece of advice would you give to a new trader?

Read Mark Douglas book "Trading in the zone". http://www.newtraderu.com is also a good resource for a new trader.

@Zozotrader

Day-trader Swing-trader stream has charts market info to help others Not investment advice Lead trader @thetradexchange Moderator / Trader @greatstockpix

Website:

https://thetradexchange.com

Email:

zozotrader@yahoo.com

How long have you been active investing or trading in the financial markets?

20 years

What year did you become active on Twitter?

2011

Services offered:

The Trade X change, is a new style of trading service that's a hybrid room of news and stock trading at a very reasonable price of 39.95/ month.

Which markets and instruments do you trade?

I trade individual Securities and ETFs, and I will also trade inverse ETFs. The markets I trade are Nasdaq and NYSE.

Why did you choose these markets?

I want stocks with volume and liquidity. I mostly trade individual names and look for relative strength in sectors, and generally trade to the long side in my trading.

What type of trader do you consider yourself?

Momentum Trader, Swing Trader, and Day Trader.

Do you have a target for your average annual returns?

No

What time frame do you prefer to trade in, and do you ever change time frames?

I trade 1-minute, 2-minute, 5-minute, and 15-min chart time frames. I try to turn day trades into swing trades if enough of a cushion is built up in the day trade.

What is the maximum drawdown you are willing to tolerate in pursuit of these returns?

100.00 to 200.00 per trade.

What technical indicators do you use to help quantify buy and sell signals?

I like to play base breaks to upside or downside. I have various moving averages on different time frames and I use vwap and pivot points also.

Are there any chart patterns you use for trading?

I use base breaks, mostly flags.

What was your best and worst trading year and what did you learn?

My worst years were 2004 to 2007. I was more of a gambler in my trading. I had the day trader bug, big bets on poor control. My trading improved after 2007, because I treated my trading more as a business, became more selective, took the gambling out of trading by staying away from earnings plays prior to the report, my trading improved.

How do you quantify your entry into a trade? What parameters do you use?

I want a stock with recent news or a sector in favor for that day. I'm looking for consolidation and a level that I feel puts bulls or bears in control of that individual stock, such as a base break up or down. I look for the level that puts the buyers or sellers in control of that stock and lean my trade to get the move up or down.

How do you manage your exit from a trade? What parameters do you use?

For Day trading, depending how the market action is that day, I like to sell in 1/3rd's. If it's a gap up morning trade, I will take the whole trade off, usually immediately to start with gains for the day to build up a cushion.

What is your favorite trading quote?

"To improve is to change; to be perfect is to change often." -Winston Churchill

What are your favorite trading books?

"Trading in the Zone" by Mark Douglas

Who are your favorite traders to follow on Twitter?

@SJosephBurns, @Chatwithtraders, @TradeHawk, @ACInvestorBlog, @Traderstewie, @Greatstockpix, @ChessNwine, and @Alphatrends.

Who has influenced you the most on your trading journey?

This is a tough one. I think I have absorbed so much from so many, but the traders that emphasized these principles helped: treat trading like a business, be in control, wait for the setup to come to you, you don't always have to be in a trade, and control your emotions.

What lessons have the markets taught you about yourself?

At the start of my trading I was very reckless, but I finally gained control. I think it was the excitement of starting to trade and being your own boss, but as you lose and do more gambling than trading, you have to change. I was able to right the ship, see my flaws, and correct them. You must learn from your mistakes and adapt.

What lessons have the markets taught you about other traders and investors?

Most traders (and I was one when starting out) want to make a killing in the market. They come in with the mindset that they don't need a plan and just buy and it will do what you want it to do. Most traders lack control and treat trading like gambling.

What do you love about trading?

I love trading because if I'm good that day I can get done quickly and not have to trade the rest of the day. Trading has become a job to me, one that I want to finish as fast as possible each day and keep my gains. Folks say you gain freedom from being a trader, but you are always thinking about it; a new setup or style. Each day is a new day, it's like a chess game each day.

What do you find to be the most difficult aspect of trading?

When I get emails from traders for help and they tell me about their losses, I then have to tell them stop trading while we sort this out, because you have to stop trading to heal. Some can stop but many can't because they're in gambling mode and feel they can't be defeated. But these traders blow up their accounts and I hate that.

What are the biggest mistakes that lead to a trader's unprofitability?

They have lack of control. They can't stop trading to turn their gambling mentality into business mentality. Feeling they always have to be trading something. Can't sit on their hands and wait for the setup.

What one piece of advice would you give to a new trader?

You are a new trader. You're supposed to have losing trades in the beginning because you're trying to discover what type of trader you are. When you first start, don't try to make a living off trading. You're a student learning. Don't take a big share size when starting to trade. Keep a job at night and trade during the day. By keeping a job, you take pressure off yourself, which is a must. Control is the biggest issue. Try to find out what trader you want to be and learn all you can while you have a paycheck coming in.

We would like to say a special thank you to all the traders that took the time to participate in this book and share their experiences with new traders—you're the best of the best.

Visit NewTraderU.com and join other traders just like you!

In the New Trader 101 e-course, you'll get:

-13 high quality videos covering how and why to trade

-Real trade examples with detailed charts

-An active member forum with hundreds of ongoing conversations

Did you enjoy this book?

Please consider writing a review.

Read more of our bestselling titles:

New Trader 101

Moving Averages 101

Trading Habits

Buy Signals Sell Signals

So You Want to Be a Trader?

Calm Trader

Investing Habits

Made in the USA
Columbia, SC
01 October 2020